A Promise to Astrid is a small book but will leave a big impact on readers ... an emotional and humorous book that readers will enjoy ... his thought-provoking storytelling shines through to readers. A Promise to Astrid is a powerful work of Christian non-fiction.
—Hollywood Book Review

A Promise to Astrid is a poignant and touching story of a special woman who gave of herself when she was facing the biggest battle of her life. We are more than pleased to award this inspiring book our "Faith- Friendly" Seal for ages 12-plus and it has also received 5 of 5 Doves for quality.
—Dove Awards

A Promise to Astrid is a touching and humorous short story that will leave a lasting impression on readers ...it will be a treasured addition to any reader's spiritual collection.
—BookWorks Review

National Pacific Book Awards
Winner 2014 Christian Non-Fiction

Dove Awarded (5 doves)

BookWorks Book of the Week, September 2015

A Promise
to Astrid

A true story

MICHAEL K. TOURVILLE

Burning Bulb
PUBLISHING

A Promise to Astrid
By **Michael K. Tourville**

Burning Bulb Publishing
P.O. Box 4721
Bridgeport, WV 26330-4721
United States of America
www.BurningBulbPress.com
www.AstridFilm.com (film website)

Cover designed by Dorian Cleavenger and used in cooperation with JC Films.

Third Edition.

Paperback Edition ISBN: 978-1-948278-14-0

Printed in the United States of America

AUTHOR'S NOTE

Ten percent of the author's profits will be donated equally between Autism Speaks and the Westover Pantry to benefit the families of military reservists stationed at Westover Reserve Base in Chicopee, Massachusetts.

With special dedication to my Dad, Bill Tourville, who recently lost his battle with cancer. Bill was well loved by his family and friends and all who knew him miss him dearly.

ACKNOWLEDGMENTS

I would like to thank my talented illustrator Bill Tourville, who happens to also be my son, and a special thank you to my Mom, Paige Tourville for all her ideas and advice. Also, my sincere appreciation goes to Niesa Rustad, Astrid's sister-in-law, for her clarification of certain facts and photos of Astrid, to Christine Chagnon for her recollections and the picture of Astrid and her Mom (DD), and to Irene Light for her early edits and suggestions. And it was my fortune to work with Cindy Calzone as a final editor, with her outstanding efficiency and her attention to detail. Also, thank you to all those friends and family members, too many to mention individually, who read earlier drafts and graciously offered their honest opinions. Everyone's input was more valuable than I can express.

PREFACE

When asked what the book is about, I still struggle for a concise but meaningful answer. It's a true story about our wonderful neighbor named Astrid who decided to help our family in ways that defy normal explanation. In a sentence, that's what it's about. As accurate as that description is, it falls pathetically short and does not convey the real meaning behind *A Promise to Astrid*. I overheard one friend ask another the same question, and the answer was, "Hmmm, well ... You'll have to read it to see." Nice enticement, but obviously leaves the question unanswered. So, what is the book really about?

The early drafts of this manuscript depicted a factual account of events that transpired over 30 years ago with our neighbor, Astrid Nicosia. This happened, then that happened, and wasn't she nice. It was a little flat and sounded more like a documentary. Something was missing. While sex, violence, conflict, and heavy drama are in fact missing from this book, none of these was the critical omission.

Writing this story was a process of gradual discovery, like drawn-out therapy sessions. Immersing myself in the project, I felt transplanted right back in the moment, exhuming memories and emotions from a long ago sealed vault. As the words began to pour out, so did feelings of anxiety, confusion, and confliction. I laughed, cried, and sometimes just sat still, amazed at the wonder of it all. More importantly, those introspective interludes gave me a chance to finally understand and fully appreciate how Astrid's actions have affected my life. In retrospect, it was there all along, subconsciously, for all these years. The advantage from a later perspective is seeing the whole story in its entirety. In the midst of things happening quickly around us, we react to what we know at the moment. When everything occurred over thirty years ago, many of the events of this story seemed independent of each other. The benefit of hindsight provides clarity, and we now see how everything tied together so neatly and was so perfectly choreographed by Astrid.

What Astrid had done for us was nothing short of miraculous, but on a larger scale, I believe her influence reaches immeasurably farther than we'll ever know. I hope in some way I was able to bring Astrid back to life, so the reader gets to know her or is reminded of someone special in their lives.

Perhaps in getting to know Astrid, my further hope is that some may feel inspired to continue what Astrid had begun. My job, as the writer, was to deliver an enjoyable and entertaining story, and hopefully convey a meaningful and inspiring message. The underlying meaning, in my opinion, is best left to the readers to interpret. The implication here is that it will evoke diverse opinions, interpretations, or beliefs, and of course, critical review, all of which I willingly accept. At the very least, I hope you enjoy the book. And if that's all it's about, then that's ok by me.

FOREWORD

As I reflect on my almost thirty years of parish ministry, I can identify certain people from each parish in which I've served who gave of themselves to others in everyday thoughtful and generous ways. Indeed, these are special folks who allow God to work through their lives in reaching out to others in simple, unassuming, yet meaningful, ways. They are, in fact, God's angels on earth. Astrid can be counted among them.

Michael Tourville has written a beautifully told true story of a neighbor who, quietly, yet powerfully, impacted his life and the lives of others. This is a heartwarming, feel-good parable of selfless giving and grateful receiving. Michael's creative choice of descriptive words enables the reader to readily get to know Astrid as if she were our neighbor as well.

Someone once said that "coincidences are God's way of remaining anonymous." God worked through his angel Astrid in a series of meaningful "God-incidences" and she served as a model to Michael and others of caring, giving, and loving.

May we all be so blessed to know an Astrid in our lives. I thank Michael Tourville for sharing Astrid's story with us and, in so doing, encouraging us to fulfill the promise made to Astrid to help others whenever we can.

The Rev. Scott Seabury, Rector
St. Christopher's Episcopal Church
Chicopee, Massachusetts

SUMMER

When we lose one blessing,
another is most unexpectedly given it its place.

—C.S.Louis

THE ACCIDENT

No one else would be calling this late. I should have left the office hours before, which meant it could only be one person. The ringing seemed amplified, as if the phone itself was shouting at me to pick up. I naturally assumed my wife Cindy was a little annoyed at my thoughtlessness, and our two young boys, Billy and Nick, were anxious for me to arrive home. It was a warm summer night in early July 1986, and here I was wasting valuable family time at work. Anticipating Cindy's displeasure, I closed my eyes, took a deep breath, and picked up the phone.

I didn't even say hello. Never had the chance. The instant the receiver was lifted, I heard Cindy's frantic voice telling me she had just been in a car accident.

Still shaken, she explained in an overly excited, rapid-fire delivery:

"Mike the guy hit my car hard and I didn't see him and he went through a red light because mine was green and the car is smashed and the guy in the van didn't tell the truth!"

Each word ran into the next in one continual exhaling stream of information until she ran out of breath.

"All right, calm down," I said. "Where are you?"

I managed to get a word in, but it only served to allow Cindy a much-needed oxygen recharge. She normally talked fast, but she was setting new speed records here.

"I'm home the cops gave me a ride the car was towed and he lied to the cop because both lights can't be green so they gave me a ticket instead of him and then . . . "

My mind was working as quickly as possible to process this information in split seconds. It was like trying to put a jigsaw puzzle together while the pieces are being tossed at you. I forcefully wedged in a few questions to break her relentless crescendo.

"Cindy, slow down. Are you alright? Are the boys with you?"

"I'm fine," she said in a more composed manner. "Billy and Nick were at the neighbor's house, they weren't in the car."

"Ok, I'm coming home right now."

By the time I got home, Cindy was able to calmly explain what had happened. A van had raced through a red light and crashed into Cindy's small 1980 Dodge Omni hatchback. The damage to her car was extensive, but fortunately, she wasn't hurt. The driver of the van insisted his light was green, hoping the police would cite her and not him, and his plan worked.

I asked Cindy why she didn't tell her version to the police at the scene. She said she was nervous, and that the guy in the van was huge with an awful menacing look on his face. "I was scared and couldn't think straight," she said. "Everything happened so fast."

Those details didn't seem so critical at the time though, because the mere fact that Cindy came out of this accident without injury was a miracle. The driver couldn't have aimed any better; if a target was painted on the center of Cindy's door, he'd have hit a bulls-eye. The car was damaged completely beyond repair, but Cindy didn't have a scratch on her.

A few days later, I went to the police station to dispute her citation. Going through a red light and causing an accident was a serious violation and we didn't want that on her record. Cindy is honest to a fault, and I knew she told me the truth about what really happened. She did not deserve a ticket for driving through a green light and finding herself in the path of a reckless driver.

The officer patiently listened to my entire argument, along with diagrams of the scene, and eventual pleas for reversal of the ticket. Before he could answer, I asked what steps we need to take in order to appeal the ticket. Politely and patiently allowing me to finish, he flatly said, "Well, what you say makes perfect sense, but your wife obviously doesn't feel so strongly about fighting the ticket."

I was puzzled. "What do you mean?"

"Looks like she sent a check and paid the ticket. I think this case is closed."

When I got home I asked Cindy why she sent a check right away. "You know," she said, "I don't like having things not paid, and on the back of the ticket it said we had to pay within twenty days. I didn't want it to be late and get in trouble."

"Yes, that is one option," I acknowledged. "But Cindy, there is another choice. One that says if you want to dispute the ticket, check this box."

"Uh oh," she said, "Does that mean . . .?"

"Yes, that's what it means. Paying a ticket is an admission of being at fault."

"Oh no," she said, "I'm sorry." She shook her head, dropping her forehead into her hands saying, "Why did I do that?"

Up until then, I had admired Cindy's ability to pay our bills so promptly. Not this time.

Mike, Billy, and Nick.

THE YOUNG AND THE SLEEPLESS

Cindy somehow managed to keep our household bills up-to-date, which was quite an accomplishment, given our ever-increasing monthly obligations exceeded our monthly income. In a constant juggling act to pay Paul from Peter's money, we relied on our hard work and a little creativity. We were ecstatic when we were able to refinance our mortgage all the way down to 10%, saving us about $125 a month. Two years before, we had purchased our house for $49,000 and were finally able to get rid of the 14.25% interest rate. We were thrilled at 10%, which was as if we'd won the lottery.

Billy was in kindergarten, while Nick, three years younger, was at home. If Cindy were to get a full-time job, we'd have to pay for Nick's daycare, and still find someone to be home for Billy after school. We simply couldn't afford the cost of full- time daycare as there weren't any jobs that paid well enough to make it worth it.

While adding up our bills one evening, Cindy had a bright idea. "What if," she said, with a rare pause to collect her thoughts, "What if I run a daycare here in the house?"

"Where?" I asked, "We don't have any room."

"We can clean out the basement, get a carpet, make a playroom, a nap room, and get some toys and . . ."

She went into great detail as if she'd planned it out for months. Maybe she had, and was finally expressing her suppressed idea. The first thing I thought of was the disruption in the house; more kids running around, more toys to trip over, more commotion, and less privacy. I wasn't completely against the idea, but needed time to process the pros and cons.

Cindy logically pointed out that running a daycare would kill two birds with one stone; she could earn an income and watch Nick at the same time, relieving us from the cost of daycare.

Since she had worked in a pre-school before and was an absolute natural when it came to taking care of children, there wasn't much of an argument from me. Besides that apparent fact, it made perfect economic sense.

In a short time, we were running a daycare in the house and it turned out to be a tremendous help. The children Cindy cared for ranged from three months to five years old, and all of them took to her like a second mom. Cindy was home when Billy came home from school, and we never had to think about daycare for Nick.

Cindy, without trying, always made her presence known, and no one ever had to wonder if she was in the room, in the house, or even within a hundred yards. It wasn't her dominating or assertive personality, and it certainly wasn't her petite frame that caught everyone's attention.

What separated Cindy from everyone else was her off-the-chart energy level and an unequaled gift of gab to match. In terms of words per minute, Cindy could outperform the best auctioneer around. The Energizer bunny was her quieter twin. If anyone attempted to keep up with Cindy, my advice was to concede early.

 In her compulsion to stay busy, Cindy found part-time work as a salesperson for a company called House of Lloyd. Here again was another dual-purpose income generator; commissions earned, plus free or discounted merchandise that came in handy for Christmas and birthday gifts. One year, Cindy's hard work was rewarded with an all-expense paid trip to Hawaii. I wasn't able to make the trip, but my grandmother happily took my place.

My job at Mass Mutual was going well, but the income still fell far short of our requirements. As a manager in the Environmental Services Department, I coordinated the activities of the housekeeping staff, which meant sticking around occasionally at night. A friend in the cleaning business offered me part-time work, which included cleaning an insurance agency two nights a week, and special projects for occasional weekend work.

The weekends consisted of late night hours, early morning hours, and around-the-clock hours (always when the businesses were closed.)

The money was helpful, but the schedule unsustainable. With both of us working two jobs, every single minute was consumed with work or attending to the boys, which left little time or money for socializing with friends. We had no spare cash; our part-time income was inconsistent, and therefore unreliable. Every dollar coming in was allocated, and any disruption of cash flow would cause acute anxiety and sleepless nights.

An unforeseen incident such as a broken appliance, car repair or any loss of income, would put us in quite a predicament. We certainly could not be prepared to deal with the aftermath of an untimely car accident.

Compounding the problem, our inexperience in certain matters led us to make a few dumb decisions and bad judgments that cost us money we didn't have. To put it another way, we were young and stupid. Some things needed to change, and they were about to. In ways we never imagined.

Mike, Cindy, Billy, and Nick, circa 1986.

THE MOST EXPENSIVE
LICENSE PLATE IN THE WORLD

The insurance company said they'd be sending an adjuster to evaluate the damage to the car and assured me we had adequate replacement coverage. I had no reason to question it, so we patiently and naively waited for them to get back to us as the days and weeks went by.

In mid-August, they finally said the repairs were extensive enough to be considered a total loss. In order to process the claim, they asked us to turn in the license plate from the car, which was still at the wreckage yard. That didn't make sense to me, but not wanting to hold anything up, at the end of the day I quickly drove down to get it.

The man at the junkyard stood at the gate with his arms folded, scanning the area like a prison guard. One look at him and I knew his sole mission in life was to terrorize anyone in his way. I told him what I was looking for and he hastily grabbed the police report from my hands.

As he looked over the information, his enormous body swelled and wheezed with every breath in the hot sticky August afternoon. An untrimmed beard sprouted from just below his eyes, covering every inch of his face. His nostrils flared when he inhaled to take in as much air as he could to fill those monstrous lungs before shouting out, "You want your car? You gotta pay!"

Startled by his voice, I stepped back. From the safety of several feet away, I said, "I don't want the car, it's a total wreck. All I need is the license plate."

"You don't take a damn thing off that car until you pay the bill!" His voice was loud and gruff – he didn't talk so much as growl at me.

"What bill?" I asked.

Slowly removing the soggy cigar from his mouth, enabling him to spit out a mouthful of wet tobacco, he answered, "Towing and storage. It's been fifty days in storage, and at twenty dollars a day, that's one thousand dollars . . . plus thirty-five dollars for towing – that bill!"

"What?" I asked, "A thousand thirty-five? I can't pay that!" I was shocked and wondered why he was so miserable. "My insurance will pay the bill later," I said. "All I need is the license plate."

"I don't give a crap about what you need," he bellowed. "No money, no license plate. And if you want it today, you've got a half hour."

At four thirty in the afternoon, the bank was about to close, and I had to get resourceful in a hurry. Between our bank account and some household cash, I scrounged up one thousand dollars. I hastily told Cindy not to worry about our depleted bank account because the insurance company would be sending us a check soon. Any day now, I assured her.

Racing against the clock, I arrived back to the junkyard with only a minute to spare. "Here's a thousand dollars, can I get the plate now?"

"Nope," he blurted out. "The bill is one thousand thirty-five. You only have one thousand," he smugly replied, while sliding the cash back at me across the table.

"You won't take a thousand dollars cash?" I held the money up in full view as a desperate plea for acceptance.

He leaned closer, enough to kindly share his nauseating cigar breath, saying, "The bill is one thousand thirty-five dollars, that's what I told you, not a penny less!" Through the cloud of smoke, saliva spewed out with every word. His intentional intrusion of my personal space was so offensive I practically tasted every repulsive odor from his body. More disgusted than intimidated, I backed away. Dismissively waving his hand, he told me to come back when I had the whole amount. Then he barked out one more demand; "Tomorrow bring me one thousand fifty-five!"

I heard him clearly but didn't give him the satisfaction of an acknowledgment. "Don't forget," he hollered out as I walked away, "I'll need twenty dollars more for one more day of storage." The smug grin on his face showed how much pleasure he derived from tormenting me.

I wanted to punch this guy in the face. But the last thing I needed was to get beat up in a junkyard. Things were bad enough without adding more to our troubles.

The next day I showed up with exactly one thousand fifty-five dollars and watched him count each bill slowly and deliberately. Then he counted a second time, just for the sheer delight of prolonging my torture.

The hefty price now paid, I was granted the privilege of walking through the highly secured graveyard of junked cars. Spotting our banged up white Omni in the far corner of the lot, I was reminded of how lucky Cindy was to have escaped without injury.

While removing the license plates, I noticed we still had some of our things left inside on the seats. I was in no mood to leave one single item of value in that car – everything I could fit my arms around was coming back home with me.

First, Nick's car seat was unbuckled. Next, two baseball caps went on my head. With one of my arm's threaded through Cindy's jacket sleeve, I gathered coloring books, crayons, and cassette tapes – even the loose change on the floor. The trunk contained beach chairs, a blanket, and a set of jumper cables. If I could have taken the tires off, I would have.

Carrying everything in one trip was no easy task, but I was determined, angry, and admittedly, a bit irrational. It became a matter of principal – not having any of our "stuff" in that man's possession. I consolidated as much as possible into one portable package; the jumper cables looped around my neck, crayons and change stuffed in my pockets, and the license plates tucked in my belt. This left both arms free to carry the car seat, beach chairs, and an old beach blanket. Between my fingers were Cindy's cassette tapes, and the coloring books clenched between my teeth.

To any passerby I must have appeared pretty pathetic; somewhere between a desperate runaway and a homeless person carting around all their essential belongings. With all this precious property precariously perched on my body, my grip wouldn't last the long walk back to the truck.

Walking carefully past the gate of the impenetrable fortress where the guard's distrustful eyes watched my every step, one of Cindy's cassettes slipped through my fingers. Any attempt to pick it up meant spilling everything else, so I kept going. After tossing everything into my truck, I stomped back to get the cassette, bent over and swiped it off the ground with an attitude, firmly denying Mr. Bluto any chance of listening to ABBA's greatest hits, as if to say, *Take THAT Mister, I'll show you!!* It's amazing how foolish and petty you can appear when someone gets you so riled up.

A few days later, the insurance company gave us the wonderful news that we didn't have the coverage for vehicle replacement, towing or storage. The accident was our fault, according to the police report, and there was the paid ticket, removing any further doubt. Had the accident been the fault of the other driver, we'd have been covered. So sorry for that, they added, just oozing phony sincerity. How could I have been so stupid? I drained all our resources for that useless license plate, and we didn't have any money left. My naivety made a bad situation much worse.

I recalled what my tenth grade English teacher once told me after being the recipient of a few classmates' practical jokes: *Mike, I admire your gullibility; it means you trust people.* Today, she might put it differently: *Mike, I'm embarrassed by your gullibility; it means you haven't grown up yet.*

ASTRID

A week or so later, on a sunny Saturday afternoon, I was playing in the backyard with Billy and Nick. At only five and two years old, they needed to be closely watched, and I alternated between playing with them and getting yard work done. It was a typical summer day that might have been lost in memory, but this day would be different and is etched in my mind forever. I noticed our neighbor Astrid watching me like a hawk, and wondered what was occupying her mind as I felt her eyes upon me wherever I went.

Over the previous two years, we had gotten to know Astrid and her husband Dominic as neighbors and as members of St. Christopher's Episcopal Church. An intimate community church where everyone knows each other, St. Christopher's was nestled in a neighborhood just over a mile from our homes. Astrid was an early riser, usually in complete harmony with the sun, and typically attended the eight o'clock service. More often, we needed the extra time in the morning and would see Astrid on her way out of church as we arrived for the later service at ten.

The first thing you noticed about Astrid was how tall and distinguished she was; she had a stately way about her with golden hair that seemed to radiate above her head. Her narrow face and sharp features were softened by sparkly blue eyes and a captivating smile that instantly drew you in with a rapturous effect. Astrid always seemed to be dressed up, no matter where she went; to church, a casual visit with friends, or a quick trip to the grocery store. With endless energy, even at eighty years old, Astrid meticulously tended to her garden every day. She dressed well for that occasion too; usually wearing a dress with a light sweater and nylons. With a quick change from her gardening shoes, she was ready for any occasion.

Astrid's strength and versatility were astounding; delicately pruning flowers one minute, and pushing full wheelbarrows of dirt across the yard the next. Without any rest, she'd start rearranging boulders and transplanting bushes in her constant quest to enhance nature's beauty. Astrid never stopped moving.

The garden in Astrid's backyard was quite elaborate; random paths with tiers separated by rocks, stones, and colorful flowers. Her tranquil sanctuary was like a mini Garden of Eden, abstract and natural – the way God would have made it. Birds sang, squirrels scurried about, and bunny rabbits happily hopped along. The only thing missing from this picture was a permanent rainbow.

We would often see Astrid and Dominic having tea at the little bistro table in the midst of her beautiful garden. On Saturdays, they were often joined by the minister from St. Christopher's Church, Father John. He had a great sense of humor - a little on the edgy side – and I would always appreciate him stopping by after the visit with Astrid to share a few of his latest jokes – usually ones you wouldn't hear at church, or certainly not over tea with Astrid!

Our homes, barely forty feet from each other, sat on identical quarter acre lots with parallel streets running in front and behind. The street in front was busy, leading to the main gate of Westover Air Force Base a half mile east. The narrow quiet road that ran behind our properties allowed for easier and safer access in and out of the driveways which were located in the back.

From the front, Astrid's home was to the left, on the east side of ours. The houses were cookie cutter replicas of each other, both late 1950's cape-style homes with small dormer windows on the second floor.

The rear view was quite different, however, where Astrid's serene environment was a glaring contrast from our backyard full of kids' things; a swing set, swimming pool, basketball hoop, bicycles, and toys.

Straddling the property line, and running the full length from front to back was a tall dense row of overgrown lilac bushes. They had grown through and around the short picket fence making the fence barely visible. About halfway down the property line, the white fence emerged through the tangled bushes into an eight foot gap and later buried itself back into hiding on the other. It was like a portal carved out of a wall of lilacs. Besides providing a neighborly view, this "gateway" was an inviting little spot that seemed to say, "Meet me here." We'd often chat over that little wooden fence that divided our two distinct worlds. I still remember Astrid's high-pitched voice with a trace of her Norwegian accent still remaining.

"Michael . . . Michael!" she called me over to the fence. "I have a question for you." I walked over, wondering what was on her mind. "Why are you selling your truck?" she asked as she pointed to the for-sale sign in the back window of my Toyota pickup truck.

Not wanting to talk about it, I chose not to explain the situation in any detail and succinctly summed it up in one sentence: "Cindy was in an accident so we need to sell my truck to afford another car."

I was exhausted, depressed and embarrassed by the whole set of circumstances, and had no desire to discuss this unfortunate calamity that we brought upon ourselves. However, Astrid's persistent questioning led me to further explain. She asked what we were buying and I said we weren't sure. I told her we had to first see what we'd get for the truck, then find out what loan we'd qualify for before deciding how much to spend. I tried to wrap up the conversation by saying everything was uncertain, but we would figure things out. I didn't tell her any details, because frankly, I didn't know any.

"Oh, don't get a loan," she said. "I would rather you didn't do that. And don't sell your truck either."

"I feel the same, Astrid, I would rather not."

"Then I will help you!" Suddenly excited by this opportunity, she spoke like a little girl eager to be chosen for a game, "Oh, please let me help!" she said, bouncing up and down with childlike enthusiasm.

"Oh no, no, but thanks for offering." I quickly replied while trying to keep a straight face.

Where in the world did this strange behavior come from? And what the heck was she thinking? I wondered. It was so out of character for Astrid, I was completely caught off guard and hardly knew what to say. As she spoke, I couldn't help looking over at her and her husband Dominic's matching blue early 1970's VW beetles.

One of them was usually in the shop getting fixed, and I wondered why she would even think of helping us before getting a new car herself. We always knew when Astrid's car was coming or going, it reminded me of an amplified version of the sound of baseball cards flipping against the bicycle wheel spokes when we were young. No other cars sounded that way, except the VW Beetles.

"Oh, but I insist!" she continued, pulling me back from my distractive thoughts. "I've helped people before, and I want to help you. Please let me do this!"

Through my expressions of doubt and amusement, she realized I wasn't taking her seriously. Her giddy expression turned stern and resolute. She wasn't bouncing up and down anymore.

"Michael, I've helped people buy homes before so I can certainly help you buy a car. That's it, my decision is made."

I was taken aback by her sudden serious mood. Not wanting to argue or offend our wonderful, but apparently delirious neighbor, I chose to humor her instead. "Ok, Astrid, thanks. That would be nice. Alright, bye now." I hoped I didn't appear too condescending. I shamefully remember rolling my eyes while walking away.

Later, over dinner, I mentioned the conversation with Astrid to Cindy. She naturally asked me what Astrid meant by helping us, and I said I had no idea. I told Cindy the only question Astrid asked was why I was selling the truck, and after that, she seemed insistent as if she was on some sort of mission. We were both amused at Astrid's willingness to help without having any knowledge of our circumstances. She had no idea of how much we'd be spending on another car (nor did we at the time), or anything at all about the license plate fiasco. But that wasn't really the point that concerned us.

Astrid and Dominic lived very modestly, actually more on the frugal side, and we thought maybe we should be the ones helping them. How her old rusty car even made the short trip to church every week was questionable.

Of course, Cindy and I didn't take Astrid seriously at all and laughed about the silliness of the whole exchange. Our attention quickly turned to more important matters of the day, like figuring out how to work the VCR we borrowed from my parents so we could watch a rented video. We forgot all about the earlier nonsense and expected Astrid would too.

Dominic and Astrid, circa 1974.

THE ENVELOPE

Early Sunday morning, at a little after six, we were suddenly awakened by a loud persistent knocking at our front door. Barely awake, Cindy ran downstairs, saw Astrid standing at the front door, and thought maybe there was an emergency. Astrid handed Cindy an envelope and said "Give this to Michael," and quickly walked away without saying another word. Cindy came back to bed and tossed me the thick envelope.

Curious, but still half asleep, we opened it to find a stack of cash: ones, fives, tens, twenties, and some fifties. The grand total: $1,741. No note. No explanation. We were shocked, and wondered, *Where in the world did she get that kind of cash so early on a Sunday morning? And why such an odd amount?* For a moment, we thought we might be dreaming. So many puzzling questions ran through our heads. *Did she lose her mind and decide to give us her cookie jar savings?*

None of that really mattered anyway, as we agreed not to accept her money and to return the envelope right away. I got dressed, neatly placed all the cash back in the envelope, and confidently marched to her house on a mission. When I knocked at her door she acted completely surprised, as if she had no clue in the world why I might be at her house at six-thirty a.m.

"Good morning, Michael!" She said so cheerfully. "How are you?"

"I'm fine Astrid, but I need to talk to you. We can't accept the—."

Pretending not to hear me, she spoke before I could finish, "How are the boys?"

"They're fine, but—."

With complete disregard to anything I had to say, she continued. "Oh good, they're such little angels." Hmmm... I had to think about that one. Little devils crossed my mind, but I wasn't about to correct her.

Jumping right to another topic, she said, "Would you like to try some chocolates?" Astrid always had a box of chocolates hanging around the kitchen, and normally it was impossible to escape without a sampling. Now it seemed impossible to get to the point.

"No thanks, too early for me," I said, politely maintaining my composure. "I haven't even had my coffee yet."

"Ok, but they're really good!"

"Astrid, I need to talk to you." This was getting ridiculous, and seemed like a little game with her. Enough of her diversions, I thought. Losing patience, I pressed on. "When you said you wanted to help, this is not what we expected. We want to return –"

"Michael, I need to ask you something." She knew how to interrupt with authority that you didn't dare defy. "I am asking you a favor; will you promise me one thing?"

"Yes, what is it?" My thinning patience didn't matter to her at all.

"Regarding our discussion yesterday and what you are here about this morning, you cannot ever bring this topic up in front of my husband Dominic. Promise?"

Concerned that she didn't want Dominic to know about their now empty cookie jar, I wasn't sure how to respond. My pointless pondering over this unexpected question was no match for her unflinching gaze.

"Sure," I said. "I promise." As if I had a choice.

"Ok, good," she said, and instantly called her husband into the kitchen. "Dominic, Michael came to say good morning to us, would you come in here for a minute?" As he slowly shuffled in from the hall, he managed a gruff "good morning" in his Italian accent.

While he stood there looking a bit bewildered, Astrid and I looked at each other and had a little nonverbal exchange: *Astrid, you think you are so clever, don't you? You really got me!*

And her cunning little look said, *Yes, I am clever, aren't I?* Now go home.

Standing there in that awkward silence, I finally said out loud, "I'll be going home now." My purposeful stride from only minutes ago was replaced with the slow walk of a dejected and confused little boy. How was I going to explain this to Cindy?

Upon my arrival home, with the money still in my hand, Cindy naturally expressed her disappointment. She couldn't understand why I didn't just say thank you and hand the money back. *Oh, how easy she made it sound!*

Recognizing the futility of an argument, I handed her the envelope and told her to give it a try. As she briskly walked out the door in her hurry-scurry mode, my only thought was, *I can't wait to hear how this goes...*

She returned home quicker than me and even more confounded. I tried to hide my "I told you so" attitude, but at least I had some redemption in my own failure to give the money back. "That Astrid is so smart," Cindy said, conceding defeat. "She kept changing the subject, and I didn't even know what to say anymore. There was no way I could get her to take the money back – I didn't have a choice!" Yes, Cindy was spot-on with that statement. Astrid simply didn't allow any other option.

Later in the week, we went car shopping and found a used 1982 Dodge Aries station wagon. The asking price was two thousand five hundred dollars, but we still didn't know how we'd pay for it. Our attempts to sell my pickup truck were unsuccessful as it was just under a year old, and we were still upside down on the loan. There would be no money left over. In fact, we would owe a balance after a sale. One thought was to sell it anyway and get two cheaper cars with payments equal to or less than the truck loan. The problem was we couldn't afford to pay the difference of the trade-in value and the loan balance.

We gave the salesperson a deposit and asked him to be patient while we arranged financing. Without Astrid's contribution, we couldn't afford the car, but we still persisted with our attempts to get a loan from a bank. Once a loan was secured, we intended to immediately give Astrid all her money back. But we weren't getting approved for the loan and were running out of options.

The following Saturday afternoon, Astrid was in her backyard digging through and pruning her flowers as usual. I'd had a week to rehearse how to overcome her conniving ways and give the money back.

With Dominic nowhere in sight, this was my chance. There she stood; defiantly waiting at the fence, squinting her eyes, as if to say, *C'mon . . . I dare ya . . .* with a piercing Clint Eastwood gaze that threw my plan off before I was close enough to speak.

"Well?" she curiously asked. "Did you buy a car yet?"

"No, not yet, Astrid, I still need to—."

In typical fashion, she didn't allow me to finish. "You need more money, don't you?"

"Oh no," I said. "No more money. I want to talk to you about that. I don't feel right, and we're still trying to get a loan and –"

"I need to give you more!" She insisted before I could continue. I started to speak but felt an invisible force stifle me. Without saying a single word, Astrid directed me to stop talking. She had a way of looking at you that commanded your full attention. I felt a sudden stillness, as if the world behind me held its breath, waiting for Astrid's permission to exhale.

With her order of silence obeyed, she firmly said, "I know what you need. Don't argue with me." I'm not even sure if she said it out loud, but I felt it and dutifully complied. She scrunched her eyebrows and gave me a scowl that would even make Clint Eastwood back off. Such an amazing transition from that angelic glow she normally radiated.

Doing my very best to ignore her tough-guy stance, I managed to tell her we were uncomfortable accepting her money. She calmly asked if I remembered my promise not to bring anything up in front of her husband. Before giving me a chance to respond, she called Dominic over, who happened to magically appear out of nowhere. She gave me that "gotcha" smile, abruptly terminating our conversation.

Later in the evening, Cindy asked how the talk with Astrid went.

"Not so good," I said. "In fact, I made it worse. She wants to help more." I told Cindy that I hardly got a word in and it all happened so fast. A familiar theme now, Cindy's nods of empathy made me feel much better. A week before, it all seemed so silly and easily dismissed as a triviality. We now realized we were dealing with a formidable personality. I don't know what it was about every conversation I had with Astrid, but I was beginning to get a complex.

THE PAPER BAG

Labor Day weekend was here before we knew it, bringing summer to an official close. Cindy and I had a crowd of people over for a cookout Saturday, but something else was pre- occupying our minds. Billy's first day of kindergarten was a couple days away and we were a little nervous. No reason really, other than normal parental anxiety. We had planned to finish off the last of his school clothes shopping on Sunday, with stores being closed on the holiday.

Our guests left late, and by the time we put Bill and Nick to sleep and cleaned up the mess, we finally made it to bed exhausted, at about midnight.

From a deep sleep, we heard that knocking sound again at our door. Blurry eyed, I looked at the clock and saw it was a few minutes after six. Cindy was comatose, and I knew it was my turn to go downstairs. Just as I opened the door, Astrid placed a brown paper bag in my hand and was halfway across the front yard before I realized what had happened. In a blink, she had enough separation between us, as if she had created some sort of a ten-second time lapse. I vaguely remember her shouting something to Dominic, but I'm convinced that her instinctive defense mechanism kicked in.

I was quite sure he was still sleeping, while not quite sure I wasn't.

Later, reflecting on Astrid's sunrise visits, I would muse over her strategy of catching us at our most vulnerable moment. The crack of dawn is one of those times, and Astrid took full advantage of our semi-conscious state.

I brought the paper bag upstairs to Cindy and we shook it out on to the bed. The dollar bills, in varying denominations all randomly stuffed in the crinkly brown lunch bag, poured into a pile on the sheets. This time, it added up to $1,835. Here we were again with those mysterious questions. *How do you explain such an unusual amount of money? Did she scrape together the last of her savings?*

Between the envelope containing $1,741 and the paper bag filled with $1,835, we now had a total of $3,576. We were getting concerned, as this was not normal behavior.

We speculated all morning, but neither of us had any answers. Nothing made sense, which led us to question her mental stability. This conclusion was more explainable than anything else, and we wondered who we should talk to about it. Anyone acquainted with Astrid knew she was one of the most conscientious and sensible people around, so we set that theory aside. We might as well accuse Mother Theresa of theft. We'd be looked at as the crazy ones. Cindy and I imagined the reaction of people when we said, *"Oh, we have the nicest neighbor ever. She keeps showing up on Sunday mornings and gives us bags of cash."* How far do you go with that story before people start looking at you suspiciously?

The most unsettling aspect was that we were ashamed we couldn't find a way to return her money. We were also afraid, and embarrassed, to tell anyone. Without actually experiencing the overpowering resolve of Astrid, how could anyone possibly understand?

Cindy asked why I even took the bag from Astrid to begin with. "I don't know." I said. "She was there, I had the bag in my hands, and she was gone. I don't know how it happened." I wisely decided not to bring up the time lapse theory.

She was persistent. "You should have just refused to accept anything from her. You shouldn't have opened the door."

"Well, it was a bag, so I thought it was chocolates, you know ... maybe cookies or something." Astrid always had chocolates and remembering her early morning offering of a week before, it was all I could think of.

Silence. And then a frozen stare. After a few long seconds, the silence was broken, but not the stare, as she slowly repeated my words.

"Chocolates...cookies...umm...Mike?"

Although she had trouble articulating a complete sentence, what I really heard her say was, *That's about the lamest explanation I've ever heard!*

"Hey, wait a minute!" I thought I had her. "It was ok last week for you. You shouldn't criticize me this week."

"Yes, but last week I had no idea, this week you should have known." She was right. Then, to ever-so-subtly remind me of my pathetic defense of accepting the bag, she just had to say it one more time – this time with perfectly delivered condescending sarcasm: "Chocolates at six in the morning? *Really* Mike?"

I wasn't going to win any arguments that morning, so I changed the subject. We were beginning to get edgy with each other, but the truth was, both of us were equally defenseless against Astrid's spell.

We knew any attempt to return the money would do no good. In fact, the more we tried, the weirder things got. This was becoming a new pattern that we didn't care to perpetuate. Some time was needed to figure things out.

Mike, Cindy, Billy, and Nick
with Mike's truck in the background, circa 1986.

THE SIXTY-NINE YEAR PLAN

Wednesday morning was a special day; it was Bill's first day of kindergarten. Both Cindy and I drove him to school, walked him to his class, and sat through a twenty-minute orientation. We were among the few lingering parents who had a hard time leaving. The teacher attempted a few subtle hints for us to be on our way, but we both hung around wanting to watch what he did next. That's when the teacher politely, but firmly, told us, "You need to leave him here and go home." And for extra measure, "Yes, you *really* do." We both responded with a submissive "Ok" and walked out not saying a word. That was just for a minute though, as Cindy didn't stop talking the entire ride home. The voice was going but I was in my own world and didn't hear a thing. Not a word.

The next morning, before I went to work, I drove Bill to the bus stop and waited with him with the other kids and several other parents. We watched them all get on and waited until the bus drove away. A few of us commented on how strange it was to see your child being in the care of other people, especially people we didn't know, for the first time. My thoughts wandered as I walked home, thinking about how his day would be and if he would make friends. When I got home, Cindy looked out of the kitchen window and asked, "Where's your truck?" I told her it was right there as I pointed to the driveway. But it wasn't right there.

It took a second before realizing I had driven Bill to the bus stop and while lost in thought, left it there. Cindy offered a ride but it was close and I told her I'd walk. Maybe there's too much on my mind, I thought, and the walk would do me good.

It was a little chillier than expected, so before heading out I changed into a different jacket. When I got to the car a few minutes later, I reached into my pocket for the keys. No keys. I left them in my other jacket. So, here I am walking home for the second time, and then trying to sneak into the house so Cindy won't hear me. I tip-toed to where the other jacket was then I stealthily reached into the pocket and silently slid the keys out. With two steps to go, I heard Cindy.

"Mike, is that you again?"

"Uh…yeah, it's me. Just forgot something, gotta go, bye." I slipped out the door and down the street, avoiding having to admit my double dose of absent- mindedness.

The next week went by uneventfully, and to our relief, no six o'clock Sunday morning surprises at the front door. On Monday morning, September 8th, I was preparing to start off my work week extra early. Early can be a relative term and getting up early might actually be considered late to anyone up well before you. This was especially the case with Astrid. No matter what time I got up she'd be out and about sooner than me. As I walked toward my truck, I hadn't planned to see her at all, but there she was, at our usual spot by the fence, watering her flowers.

"Good morning Astrid!" I thought I might surprise her, but she acted as if she was anticipating my arrival.

"Good morning Michael! How are you?" She joyfully replied, not breaking her rhythm as she waved the showering spray hypnotically back and forth.

It seemed like such an opportune moment, a perfect time to have a serious talk about arranging to pay her back. The peace of the early morning air just seemed to tell me so. It was a perfect time – no distractions, no Dominic; only Astrid and me, and the sun sneaking over the horizon to join us.

I walked over to Astrid and thanked her for all she had done for us and told her of our intentions to get another loan and pay her back as quickly as possible. She listened as she hadn't before, without any interruptions, and patiently waited for me to finish. Her uncharacteristic behavior should have told me something was up.

Astrid turned the water off and put the hose down without a word. Turning to look me straight in the eye, signaling her full attention to the matter, she began, "Ok, Michael. Yes, you can pay me back."

I was so relieved! Actually, quite stunned at how easily she gave in. Finally, some progress! She seemed so agreeable, allowing me to control the conversation for once. Or so I thought.

"However," she paused and leaned closer to make sure I was listening. "You need to pay me back on my terms."

"Well, all right," I said. "What do you have in mind?" I was ready.

At that moment, the sun rose over Astrid's shoulder, causing me to squint. It was as if someone flipped a switch, turning on the blinding interrogation lights. I thought the sun was actually teaming up with her; a partner in her mission of persuasion, right on cue.

"Before I tell you, you need to promise that you will abide by my terms. Promise?" There was that glare in her eyes again. I felt an unexpected shift in the wind. Most likely, it was the rush of confident air escaping my lungs, like a deflating balloon.

"Astrid that depends on—"

"No, you need to promise – my terms or nothing!"

"Yes, I promise," I responded obediently, the tough negotiator that I was.

"First, I want you to pay me a dollar a week. No more than that – every week, one dollar."

"But, Astrid—" The obvious occurred to me but wasn't sure how to put it. She was eighty years old. Before I could say another word, she abruptly interjected.

"Let me finish, I've got more." Her patience waning, she took on a little attitude and wasn't going to tolerate any more interruptions. "I don't want you to start paying me until six months from now. Not a day sooner, understood?"

"Six months?"

"From today, yes. Do you understand?"

"Yes, I understand...but that will take a long time and—"

"Michael, you promised to go by my terms, and those are the terms. A dollar a week, starting six months from today, that's it."

If I didn't know her better, I'd think she was trying to be funny. Astrid obviously recognized our discomfort and found a way of turning her charity into a loan, at least as far as she was concerned. The entire idea was so absurd and really wasn't acceptable to us at all, but we had no choice. She added one more thing before turning back to her garden. "Someday if you can help someone," she said, "I know that you will. That's part of the terms too, but I think you know that already."

Well, I thought, if I was ever in the position to help someone financially, it would be a long time away.

As I backed out of the driveway I felt confused, conflicted, and once again, outsmarted. *A dollar a week... Six months from today? What just happened here?* I was convinced everything was lining up just right and within a matter of minutes, she took all the wind out of my sails. From the rearview mirror, I saw Astrid showering her flowers side to side, rhythm resumed, like nothing ever happened.

On the way to work, the morning voices on the radio rambled on while I contemplated Astrid's proposal. My thoughts were interrupted by a news story that struck me as amusing. A new national talk show was debuting this morning, they reported, hosted by a Chicago woman who would compete with the Phil Donahue Show. They went on to mention that she was in the movie The Color Purple, and I remembered her as the big tough woman, Oprah something. The story seemed sort of odd to me; it didn't fit, and she didn't seem the type for a talk show.

They said the show would cover a myriad of current events and social topics, and feature interesting guests. Well,

I thought, *I have one for you. . . I'll bet you'll never have a guest like Astrid!* Too late Oprah, you missed your chance!

All day I thought how silly it would feel to walk over to Astrid's house every week with a dollar in my hand. *Should I just give her four dollars a month? Or would she take a year's worth all at once?* I had a hard time envisioning it playing out that way.

Let's see . . . with a grand total of $3,576, it would take 3,576 weeks to pay it back, or 69 years, bringing us to the year 2055. That goes well beyond Astrid's life, my life, and perhaps my kids' lives. As preposterous as this was, our intention was to pay Astrid back the full amount as soon as possible and be done with it. *If only we knew how . . .*

With all that behind us, Cindy and I completed the car transaction we had begun a week earlier. We paid for the car, another few hundred for the registry fees, taxes, and the required up-front insurance.

Then of course, we replenished our bank account for that very expensive license plate. We added the numbers on a piece of paper to make sure we had enough to cover everything:

$ 2,200	Final cost of the car
$ 300	Registration, taxes, insurance
$ 1,055	Towing and Storage
$ 3,555	Grand Total

We never told Astrid how much the car cost, nor did we mention the towing and storage fee. Not a word. None of these things ever came up in conversation. But here we were, all set with the car and all the required fees – almost right to the dollar from the money in the envelope and paper bag together. *How did Astrid so accurately know what we needed?* We hadn't even known ourselves until the transaction was completed.

Maybe Astrid wasn't so exact after all—she was off by twenty dollars. It was funny that we had that extra twenty. It was also funny that the gas tank was empty and that's exactly what it cost for our first fill-up.

Billy and Nick in the car.

FALL

The unthankful heart deserves no mercies but the thankful heart will find in every hour, some heavenly blessings.

–Henry Ward Beecher

Billy and Nick in the backyard, circa 1986.

DOMINIC

Summer vanished and the leaves quickly began to turn color. Massive oak trees that provided a shady canopy in both our backyards rapidly let go of their leaves, blanketing everything in sight. When the last remnants of the leafy collage hit the ground, it was time to clean up before the first snowfall.

Occasionally I'd assist Astrid with a few chores here and there, but she declined most offers to help. In fact, whenever I'd ask if she needed anything, she'd politely refuse and quickly offer to help me instead. She was proud of her ability to do physical work at her age, and I fully respected her wishes. It was one thing to accept Astrid's money, but allowing her to do my landscaping would border on abuse of the elderly.

The chilly winds and shorter days signaled the onset of winter. The drive home from work coincided with the disappearing sun, leaving only the weekend days to see Astrid outside. With Dominic devotedly by her side, she spent her days puttering around her garden, a heavier jacket now draping over her shoulders. Our weekend activity, along with the rest of the neighborhood (and most of New England for that matter) was raking and bagging endless piles of leaves.

On a cool Saturday afternoon in late October, Astrid asked if I wouldn't mind allowing Dominic to help me with a few little projects in the yard. Dominic didn't move very fast; he usually shuffled aimlessly around, following or hovering over Astrid, looking for something to do.

I remember him being shorter than Astrid, and of course, a little wider too. He usually wore a week's worth of white whiskers matching the short patchy hair on his head. Dementia was setting in, and his demeanor became increasingly grumpy. Astrid saw right through his crankiness and knew it would do him good to feel useful. At this point, he was a challenge to take care of, and she managed it with extraordinary patience and dignity.

I gladly went along with Astrid's request, and when I asked Dominic to help me with a few simple odd jobs around the yard, he eagerly responded. With only a couple of minor things to do, the timing was good. In a few hours, Cindy, the boys, and I were going to my brother Dave's house to watch the Boston Red Sox play the sixth game of the World Series against the New York Mets. We all counted on the first Red Sox championship in 68 years, and I wasn't going to miss this game for anything.

Dominic and I began to repair the fence when we were suddenly interrupted by Robin, our neighbor on the other side. Robin was a little older than me, probably early thirties, and lived with her elderly parents. She started shouting and crying, and I had a hard time slowing her down enough to make sense. She kept repeating, "I think he's dead! I think he's dead!"

"What happened?" I asked.

"I told him not to go to the pool but he went anyways and he fell in and I think he drowned!"

I naturally assumed her father, who was accident prone, had fallen into their in-ground pool.

"You need to come get him out, I think he's dead. Hurry!"

I put my things down and told her I'd come. I'll admit I was a little nervous but something didn't make sense. Our pool had been covered for the season over a month ago, and I assumed theirs was too. *How could someone drown in a covered pool?*

"Hurry, run, he's just lying in the water and we can't just leave him there." She impatiently demanded.

I ran as quickly as I could, preparing for the sight of a man drowned in the murky water of the pool cover. Her father was a big man and I'd have to figure out quickly what to do when I got there. Adding to the stress, Robin tearfully exclaimed, "It's so terrible! I wish he listened to me. Why did he do that?"

We arrived at the pool. The cover was full of leaves and brown water, but no body. The pool looked relatively undisturbed.

"Where is he?" I asked.

"There, right there!" She pointed to the side of the pool.

"I don't see anyone," I replied, taking a few steps closer.

"Look!" She yelled. "See?"

"Ahh, … I do see." I conceded while closing my eyes, letting the nervous tension drain from my body. "Robin," I paused, took a breath, and continued, "It's a chipmunk."

"Yes, and he shouldn't have gone in. And now he's dead." It was now obvious to me that it made no difference if it was a chipmunk. To Robin, it was almost a pet with a personality and she was as upset as if it was a person.

"I'll get him out for you. Do you have a skimmer?" She brought the skimmer over, and I pulled out the chipmunk. I was about to toss it in the woods across the street when she stopped me and asked if I could help her bury it. Realizing how important this was to her I agreed. By then Dominic moseyed over to the scene. We found a spot, dug a hole and buried Robins' little friend. Dominic patted the top with his hands and drew a little cross in the dirt.

With the crisis over, Dominic and I returned to our tasks at home. We repaired the fence, tightened up the pool cover, and replaced the hinges on the shed doors. Seeing how proud he was to contribute, Astrid's mission was accomplished.

Recognizing Dominic's limitations, and his short attention span, we bounced from one little task to another. I thanked him and walked him across the yard before I ended up having to carry him home.

His body couldn't handle the physical exertion for long, but his face beamed with pride. And so did Astrid's. She looked at him so adoringly while he worked, almost as if they were teenagers. Knowing she was watching, he did his best to show off what remaining vigor he had left, still trying to win over her admiration.

Refusing my help to carry a fence post, he just had to demonstrate how strong he still was. The youthful expressions of love and affection passed between the two of them filled the air with a magical energy.

We finally made it to my brother's house in time to watch the World Series. How the Red Sox game turned out that night was another story and lives on as an unforgettable chapter of Boston Red Sox history.

One Sunday afternoon in early November, Astrid came running over to us in a panic looking for Dominic. She usually kept a close eye on him, but when she woke from a nap he was nowhere to be found. Astrid had slept about an hour and she worried he could have wandered off anywhere. We became more concerned when we noticed his car missing from the driveway.

Within a few minutes, our fears were temporarily relieved when we found his blue Volkswagen about a hundred yards away, parked diagonally along the side of the street. *Thank God*, we thought. *At least he didn't go far.* At a closer look, the scene was somewhat alarming. The front end of the car was against a telephone pole, but it didn't appear to be a crash. The pole was barely touching the very center of the bumper with no damage, it was as if he was going slowly along and the pole inconveniently got in his way. Dominic apparently decided to keep going anyway – without the car. The door was open, with the engine still running, but he was nowhere in sight. We brought the car home and began our search for Dominic.

After twenty minutes, we found him about a half mile away in a neighborhood, leisurely walking around without a care in the world. You never really knew what kind of a mood you might catch Dominic in - belligerent or blissful, and subject to change without notice. Fortunately, this time it was the latter and he was fully compliant when we approached him. We brought him back home safely, much to Astrid's relief. Dominic had no recollection of hitting the pole or even taking the car out at all. Needless to say, that was his last driving adventure. His keys were taken away from him just in time, as the treacherous driving season began early with an unexpected mid-November snowstorm. Thanksgiving was still two weeks away, which meant a long winter was ahead of us.

WINTER

So teach is to number our days, that we might
apply our hearts unto wisdom.

−Psalm 90:12

THE WINTER GAMES

The arrival of winter presented an opportunity to relieve some of the guilt I was carrying for accepting Astrid's money. When the next snowfall came in mid-December, I very quickly shoveled her driveway, sidewalk, and cleaned off her car. *One small victory.*

A half hour later, while starting on my own driveway, Astrid called me over from her doorway to help take her trash out. Once at her door, she thanked me for shoveling and asked if I could tie her trash bags and take them out to the curb because her arthritis was bothering her. She offered to hold on to my gloves while I tied the bags and took them to the end of the driveway.

When I came back, she very quickly handed me my gloves, abruptly said goodbye, closed her door, and disappeared. *Well, that was odd,* I thought. But again, this was typical Astrid behavior. At least she allowed me to do something for her — a rare event in itself. Putting my gloves back on while walking home, I stopped dead in my tracks. Something was in the fingers of each glove. *What the heck,* I thought. *What did she do?*

Immediately, I turned around and caught a glimpse of her looking through the window as she quickly moved away behind the curtains. Apparently, she wanted to be entertained by my reaction to her sneaky trick. I pulled out five and one-dollar bills from the fingers in the gloves and just shook my head, amused at her crafty little prank. I knew what was going through her mind: *I've outsmarted him again!* Yes, she did indeed.

We played little games like this throughout the winter months. I'd look for things to do for her and she'd try to find a way to pay me. I'd wave from a distance, knowing that an up-close encounter would mean I'd fall victim to her scheming ways. I tried not to give her any advantage to pull off any ingenious tricks. She was smarter than me, plain and simple. Every time I thought I was getting ahead, she found a way to out-maneuver me. Some imagination would be needed to one-up her, and I was determined to get even.

The opportunity came quickly. On the last Saturday evening in January, Cindy and I were out at a banquet for House of Lloyd, the company she worked for. Snow had been falling all evening but it conveniently stopped when we came home about midnight. *Perfect*, I thought. *I'll do it now, she'll never see me!*

There I was in my suit, dress shirt, and tie, shoveling by the moonlight. For some reason, I remember it being a lot of fun; maybe it was the thrill of feeling like I was getting away with something that added to the enjoyment. I went to bed quite satisfied, and my own driveway waited until the morning.

Early the next day while cleaning off the snow-covered cars in our driveway, who do I see walking toward me? Not Astrid, but her husband Dominic; cautiously approaching, and all bundled up, being extra careful not to fall in the snow. He handed me an envelope and slowly turned back home without saying anything discernible.

I wondered how long it took him to get ready for this assignment and visualized Astrid tucking in his scarf, buttoning his coat, adjusting his hat . . . and then undoing it all only minutes later.

Astrid's handwriting on the outside of the envelope explained that she wasn't feeling well and was unable to go to church this morning. She asked if we could drop off her weekly envelope, which was inside the larger one. I folded the envelope, placed it in my pocket and went inside to get ready for church.

As the collection baskets were being passed around, I remembered I hadn't taken her small envelope out of the larger one. Quickly tearing it open, I saw two envelopes inside. Along with her church envelope were a thank-you note and a twenty-dollar bill. As usual, Astrid wins again. This kind of creative competition went on all winter long. Once in a while, she would let me have my way just to prevent my self-esteem from completely caving in. I won a few battles, but she was clearly winning the war.

My efforts to erase any guilt fell far short.

THE MYSTEROUS VISITOR

The frigid weather felt like it would last forever, with a constant layer of white covering the ground. When the stubborn mounds of dirty snow finally began to melt into the mud, an occasional whiff of spring brought hope. The dormant life in Astrid's garden silently awaited her consent to re-emerge.

Astrid loved to be outside, but in the cold dark days of winter, she made rare appearances. Normally, tire tracks could be seen in the snow covered driveway, providing evidence of her daily errands and other social activities. But lately, there were none. On Sunday mornings, when we'd routinely hear the sound of her VW engine waking us up as she drove off to church, it was silent.

One day in early March a man in his mid-forties knocked at our front door and asked Cindy if we knew Astrid. After apologizing for the intrusion, he told Cindy that Astrid had been admitted to the hospital and that she had cancer. Although he didn't have much detail, he said he felt an urge to stop by and let us know.

When I came home, Cindy explained what happened, and I naturally asked who he was.

"I don't know," she said. "He didn't say."

"But how did he know we were friends with Astrid?" I asked, "Don't you think that's a little unusual? Do you know if Astrid told him?"

"I don't know, but it's obvious he didn't know how well we know Astrid because he asked about it," she said, almost irritated with my questioning. "Mike, I don't know who he was, and he said he wasn't even sure himself why he stopped by."

"Ok, so a stranger comes along, who never met us, and he just impulsively decides to tell us Astrid is in the hospital?"

"Yes, that's it," she said. "He seemed to be a nice guy and I didn't think I needed to interrogate him. We didn't have anything else to say." I had a hard time holding Cindy's attention, while she buzzed around the kitchen preparing dinner.

"Bill and Nick, come on upstairs," she shouted. "Supper's ready!"

I was about to ask another question when the phone rang. Cindy didn't skip a beat picking it up on the way back to the stove.

"Hi, Mom…Oh really? I didn't know…" Right then and there I knew my inquisition about the mysterious visitor came to an end. With the phone tucked in her neck, and the cord winding and twisting around her body, she chatted and spun around between the table and counter like a high-speed ballerina dancer. Throughout Cindy's chatty phone dance, I was talking with Bill and Nick and lost track of time, and of course, our earlier conversation. Soon Cindy found herself wound up with the thirty-foot cord and tethered to the wall with the last two remaining feet of cord. I got up to help her untangle after she finally said goodbye.

Once freed from the entanglement, she suddenly declared, "Oh, I forgot something; he said he worked on her car."

"Who?" I asked. "Whose car?"

"Astrid's car, the guy we were just talking about Mike, how could you forget so fast?"

"Oh, yeah, that guy. It was her mechanic?"

"Yes!" She exclaimed as if it was a prize-winning answer.

"Of course," I said. "Now it all makes perfect sense!"

None of this really mattered anyway. The information was enough.

SAYING GOODBYE

The next day was Friday, March 6th, our son Billy's sixth birthday We had a party planned for Saturday, so I squeezed in a visit with Astrid at the hospital after leaving work.

When I arrived at Astrid's room, I saw Father John finishing a prayer with Astrid. I stepped back, gave them a few minutes, and gave a quick knock before entering. Astrid looked surprised to see me, even a bit embarrassed. She wanted to keep her cancer diagnosis a secret and did not want anyone to know she was there. She gave Father John a look, as if he was the one who betrayed her confidence. He shook his head and held his hands up in denial, doing his best *Not me* performance. After chatting for a few minutes, he said he'd stop by the next day and said a quick goodbye.

Astid was proud and respectful, and it was important for her to dress and present herself well, wherever she was. Lying helpless in her pajamas robbed her of all that pride, frustrating her well beyond tolerance. She wanted to keep her cancer diagnosis a secret and did not want us to know she was there. It was obviously too late – a moot point really, as I sat there with her. She then asked how I knew, and I told her the truth about the visitor with no name. She shook her head in disbelief with a look on her face that said, "*You can't fool me, you'll need to try harder than that.*"

But I didn't bother trying harder because both of us knew it really wasn't that important. There were other things to talk about. The first thing that crossed my mind was how long it had been since we had seen Astrid. I just didn't know. Was it only a few weeks, maybe February, or could it have been as far back as January? We had been so pre-occupied with our daily activities that I hadn't paid any attention and could not recall. Seeing her lying there I felt embarrassed, guilty of being so oblivious and neglectful of a friend in need. Especially after all she had done for us.

Astrid appeared much older, as if years had gone by. Astrid's mind was still quick, but the spark in her eyes was gone; that sharp penetrating look that stood me at attention was now hazy and unfocused. Inflicting its malicious wrath on her body, the cancer was doing its work in a hurry.

When I asked anything about her condition or how she was feeling she changed the subject. Astrid was abnormally private about certain matters and never wanted to draw any attention to herself. She would refuse to take credit for anything, or trouble anyone for the smallest of favors. The "give" side of her scale was full, and the "take" side empty. She didn't want anyone to be inconvenienced by spending time visiting when we had "more important things to do." Somehow, incredibly, she thought her absence would go unnoticed.

During the visit, she asked how my job was going at Mass Mutual and if I knew her friend DD (as in Dee Dee) who also worked there. I said no and explained that with four thousand employees there were lots of people I didn't know. Astrid then clarified (as if it would change my response) that her name was actually Doris. She said everyone called her DD because those were her initials. I again told Astrid I was sorry I didn't know anyone by that name.

"Hmm…" She sighed, expressing disappointment. "Maybe you'll get to know DD someday," she optimistically added. "Maybe you should have lunch with her sometime." I had no idea how, or even why, I might have any reason to meet with DD, but patiently humored her. "I'm sure you'll meet one of these days," she continued, stubbornly not giving this topic up. After a few more comments about her friend, we soon changed the subject.

Astrid's energy was fading, her voice dropping to a whisper. Our conversation was interrupted by her nurse coming in to check on her.

"This is Michael, my neighbor," Astrid said, taking a labored breath before continuing. "Isn't he nice to come and see me?" Then, as usual, things got weird.

"Oh, my goodness," the nurse said. "You are Michael, the neighbor that does all those wonderful things for Astrid?"

"Umm..." I couldn't say anything, and I just looked at both of them with a blank look on my face.

"Astrid has told me all about you, shoveling and taking care of other things for her all the time. I wish I had someone like you next door to me!"

Astrid looked away, embarrassed as if she'd been caught saying something she shouldn't have. I wondered. *Did this nurse have any idea that my motivation was purely guilt driven? If she only knew what Astrid had done for us? And furthermore, how would this topic come up in conversation anyway?* With Astrid, you never really knew.

At first, I became somewhat amused to see Astrid so speechless. There was nothing she could say, but her eyes said *Ok, I'm caught – you got me.* We looked at each other, smiled, and both laughed together. Maybe it was the awkward silliness of us both being stuck with not knowing what to say, which was rare for Astrid and me, as we had a habit of interrupting each other in any normal course of conversation. The laughter disrupted her breathing, and quickly depleted her energy. A few minutes were needed for her to regain composure and resume her normal respiratory rhythm.

Astrid was beginning to drift in and out of consciousness, struggling to keep her sleepy eyes open. When the nurse left the room, it became suddenly quiet, and Astrid reached out for my hand. "Thank you," she softly whispered. "I'm glad you came." It was time to go. At that moment, I felt it was the last time I would see her. She wasn't ever coming home again and strangely, all I thought of was her garden. A tiny piece of nature would be missed by its nurturing caretaker, left neglected and undernourished. I could almost feel the collective heartbreak from the tiny animals that thrived in the tiny paradise she created for them. With nothing left to say, we shared a tearful goodbye.

Two mornings later, the first rays of the sun slowly stretched out to greet Astrid. She had managed to stay awake for one last sunrise before her heart stopped beating, and peacefully passed into God's hands. It was shortly after six, Sunday morning.

The hospital didn't notify us, nor did we expect them to. There was no obituary, and no mysterious visitors arriving at our door to share the news of Astrid's passing. It was simply a visit to an empty hospital room on Monday that confirmed the heartbreaking reality. The official cause of death was cardiopulmonary arrest, as a consequence of cancer's effect on her weakened body. According to the death certificate, as I learned much later, her cancer had been diagnosed about a year before her death. Arriving home, I walked over to our usual spot along the fence. Noticing the two Volkswagens still parked in Astrid's driveway, I was sad we wouldn't ever be hearing the clicking putt-putt sound that would announce Astrid's arrival home from a hundred yards away.

I imagined Astrid standing there and felt her presence. I could hear her voice, that sweet, distinctive voice, saying, *"Michael . . . Michael . . . Would you promise me one more thing?"* . . . Her words came back to me, *"Someday if you can help someone . . . I know that you will . . . that's part of the terms, but I think you know that already."*

That earlier assumption was now a promise. I hadn't forgotten. *Yes, Astrid, I promise . . .* and with that thought I reactively looked for Dominic to appear from around the bushes.

Behind me, the sun fell below the trees and the remaining light in Astrid's backyard faded to shadows, like heavy, tired eyelids closing shut for the last time. So many things wouldn't be the same anymore.

Over the next several days, I was reflecting on all the extraordinary events that transpired since the accident the previous summer. Then, out of the blue, I was overcome, like a sudden wave that took my breath away. I remember making an audible gasp when it hit me. Astrid passed away on March 8, and I hadn't even made the connection until that moment. She specifically told me to wait *six months* before paying her, and *not a day sooner*, as I vividly recalled. It was September 8th, six months ago to the day, when she laid out the terms of the "loan." I remembered how confident, determined and unwavering she was then. Astrid knew, right to the day, when she would pass away.

I thought about the odd amounts of money in the envelope and the little lunch bag and how it all eerily added up to precisely what we needed. She was so insistent, so steadfast, and resolute that everything would turn out just as she intended.

None of the details of our loan rejection from the bank were ever discussed with her. We still had the balance of the previous loan to pay off for the wrecked car and could barely afford that. Nothing specific was mentioned to Astrid at all.

The perfect solution orchestrated by Astrid, in spite of the *absence* of information shared, was quite a conundrum to Cindy and me.

There was never an opportunity, nor an apparent desire on Astrid's part to want to know or to even ask. I suppose she never really needed to.

SPRING

Let us be grateful to people who make us happy,
they are charming gardeners who make our souls blossom.

–Marcel Proust

Astrid and a friend, circa 1960 (top) and 1967 (bottom).

DD

About a month passed, and I still had a hard time reconciling everything. The guilt never went away.

In fact, the weight grew heavier with each passing day. To me, the thirty-five hundred dollars was a fortune, and even though Astrid was gone, that debt felt like owing a million dollars. In a strange way, it was actually worse with Astrid gone. I wondered if, or when, anyone in her family would realize what Astrid had done and then decide to inquire. Or even more problematic, ask us to return the money. How would I explain? My imagination wandered with all kinds of anxiety that I couldn't shake.

Astrid's house became a vacant and lifeless box. Once an island of vibrancy, it was now a still, conspicuous void. Astrid's closest family members lived a few hours away in New York City and began to make arrangements to sell the property. They asked if I would take care of some of the routine maintenance, just to keep the house presentable.

Cleaning the debris from the garden where Astrid spent her time brought forth a mix of emotions. I felt sad entering her backyard for the first time since she passed. Removing the smothering leaves from her garden, it was as if the soil expressed gratitude, finally being allowed to breathe again, after months of suffocation. I noticed a few tulips beginning to sprout and wondered if Astrid would be pleased. Easter was only a few days away, perfect timing for new life.

In mid-April, I had accepted a new position at Providence Hospital in Holyoke and was working out my two weeks' notice. I would miss my job at Mass Mutual, but the higher salary from the new job would provide much needed financial relief and afford us the ability to pull back on other part-time work. I had one more day to go at Mass Mutual when my office phone rang in the late afternoon. I picked it up to hear an unfamiliar voice ask "Is this Michael?"

"Yes, who is this?" I asked.

"I'm sure you don't know who I am, but I'd like to introduce myself. My name is DD."

I was still for a minute before responding. I wasn't sure I heard her correctly, "DD? Did you say DD?" She answered affirmatively and I continued. "Yes, I have heard your name from Astrid." I sensed relief from the other end.

"Oh good," she said. "I was afraid you would have no idea who I was. Astrid often mentioned you and told me some time ago that you worked here." She spoke as if scripted by Astrid herself. "I wonder if you might have time for lunch."

When those words were spoken, I froze. *Astrid is still able to do this . . . How did she know?* With so many thoughts racing through my mind, I suddenly realized I hadn't responded to DD.

"Lunch? Yes of course. I would love to meet for lunch." The very last time I was with Astrid, she had found a way to predict just one more thing.

Recalling the conversation with Astrid in her hospital room, I remembered trying to change the topic when she wouldn't stop talking about DD. It didn't seem relevant to anything and now I was feeling bad because I hadn't made any attempt to initiate contact. I couldn't help wondering why DD would have wanted to get together. I was curious though, and of course, happy to meet Astrid's friend. We made a lunch date for the very next day.

During our visit, we never left the subject of Astrid. DD informed me that Astrid was born in Norway in 1906 and came over on a ship from Oslo in 1931 when she was 25. She went through Ellis Island, made her home in New York and met Dominic when he was in the U.S. Air Force.

SS Stavangerfjord, the ship that brought Astrid to the United States.

Dominic was born in Sicily but spent his career in the Air Force. He and Astrid lived many years in Japan and Australia, where he was stationed. Finding their way back with Astrid and Dominic were lots of books, silk screens, and other types of Japanese artifacts. One special souvenir accompanied them back from Australia, a Chihuahua named Aussie. DD told me that Astrid was also an artist and wrote poetry. There were so many interesting aspects to Astrid's remarkable life; I could've listened to DD all afternoon.

When Astrid and Dominic had lived in New York sometime in the 1950's, she became a personal assistant for one of the Diebold family members (of the security systems company). In 1961, when Dominic was stationed at Westover Air Force Base in Chicopee, Massachusetts, they bought a house on Westover Rd., a two-minute drive into the base. Even after the move, Astrid remained friends with the Diebold family, and would often spend time visiting between their New York and Florida homes. DD revealed that the Diebold's had left Astrid a large inheritance. Astrid never wanted to spend the money on herself and made a point of helping people whenever she could.

I told DD that Astrid didn't appear to have a spare dime, and she laughed. "Yes, that's the way she lived. She had no use for the money. She felt happier to give as much as she could away, and that's what she did." As DD spoke, I remembered Astrid's words: *I've helped people before, and I want to help you.*

Everything was making more sense now. I didn't mention a word about our personal story with Astrid. In fact, up until that time, we hadn't told anyone at all.

I mentioned to DD that I had not seen Dominic around since February, so I asked her if she knew who was taking care of him. She said that a few weeks before Astrid was hospitalized, she had arranged for him to be moved to the Veterans Hospital located in Leeds, Massachusetts. Astrid had taken care of Dominic as long as she could, but he needed professional care and the time was right to let him go. How Astrid managed to take care of Dominic while her own illness was progressing was astonishing. She quietly and efficiently arranged everything, making sure he would be well cared for. His condition had deteriorated to the point where he wasn't even aware of Astrid's passing.

I thought of the last time I saw Dominic, plodding through the snow to deliver the envelope Astrid had given him. I also pictured Astrid watching through her window, watching his every step, with that same loving look on her face when he worked in the backyard.

My earlier curiosity prompted me to ask DD what made her decide to call. She said no real reason, other than Astrid pointing out on several occasions that two of her friends had worked for the same company and had never met. Astrid believed her friends should know each other and DD thought it was about time to meet. I told DD I was so glad she called, and that her timing was incredible because it was my last day and I was starting a new job the very next week.

"I'm not surprised," she said, pointing to the sky. "Perhaps Astrid had some influence in that!"

I thought, *Of course, she did!* There was nothing *perhaps* about the timing at all. I was getting quite used to this now.

After lunch, I felt lighter and couldn't explain why. Thinking about all that DD revealed, I knew there was a purpose. A weight was lifted; the burden of guilt I carried was suddenly gone. Like Astrid's suffocated garden, I could breathe again. I didn't really have an issue with the fact that the money for our car came from an inheritance that Astrid had intended to give away. I believe Astrid, even in her hospital bed, knew that had to be overcome. And so it was, just as she planned.

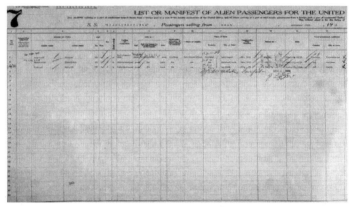

Ship manifest for SS Stavangerfjord, sailing from Oslo, November 24th 1931.

ANGELS

To one who has faith, no explanation is necessary.
To one without faith, no explanation is possible.
—Thomas Aquinas

I sometimes think about how little events often trigger bigger things. Small occurrences, tiny gestures, or decisions that seem insignificant often have a way of creating life-altering events. Some people attribute these occasions to mere coincidence, and sometimes that's true. Others say that certain outcomes are predestined culminations of a perfect plan. And when explanations don't come easily, it may simply be divine intervention at work. In my opinion, it is very simple; they are only what we *believe* they are. I wonder how often these experiences occur and we're too busy to notice or pay any attention to them.

All that transpired with Astrid has gone through my mind a million times. First, how the van driver had lied about the accident, placing fault on Cindy. Had he been honest, the series of events would have never happened. Then there was the repulsive man at the tow yard, demanding his money without a shred of compassion.

Just as we were beginning to lose faith in people, someone magical appeared, in sharp contrast to the despicable behavior we had witnessed. Astrid helped us overcome our loss of trust and faith in people. The resentment we were feeling for a few contemptible characters blew away as quickly as a passing breeze.

From the moment the For Sale sign in my truck window caught Astrid's attention, everything changed. Nothing fazed Astrid at all, she allowed nothing to impede her will. Any obstacles were easily swept away; they simply weren't worthy of her attention. She gently (and sometimes assertively) exerted her influence with those around her, and her contagious inspiration quickly became evident to us.

We're thankful for Astrid's mechanic, who felt so compelled to tell us she was in the hospital. How dreadful to have been denied the chance to say goodbye? And then, the perfect timing of DD's phone call and our enlightening visit. I can't imagine carrying those guilty feelings around forever. We're quite sure Astrid's influence extends far beyond our little circle.

Astrid's wishes were eventually granted. The debt was paid, with interest. Not to her directly, of course, but that wasn't her desire. She had a greater purpose in mind. One of the provisions of the loan was for us to help others someday, and although that "someday" took a while, her request was fulfilled.

Many years later, a few opportunities arose to satisfy Astrid's outstanding loan condition. We were fortunate to be in the position to help some friends and family members overcome serious financial difficulties. None of them ever knew where it all began. After all, it was the last promise made to Astrid, all those years ago.

That's not the end of Astrid's legacy, however. It's a story that's not supposed to end. It took me a while to realize that Astrid's garden wasn't confined to her backyard, and the soil not the only recipient of her seeds. Astrid's garden of kindness, goodwill, and generosity is still growing, and thriving in unseen places. She was a rare gift that we will treasure forever. She lived an eventful eighty years all over the world, and the last twenty-five of those years on Westover Road in Chicopee. We are grateful to have had her as a friend and neighbor for the last two of those years.

We were blessed by Astrid's presence in our lives. I have to believe that angels exist because I feel I knew one personally. She was our friend, our neighbor, our angel. Since I hadn't ever heard the name Astrid before, I was curious what the meaning was behind her name.

As is the case with most names, Astrid has several meanings. One is "Little Star." Another is "Beautiful Goddess." And lastly, Astrid means "Divine Strength" or "God's Strength." I didn't really have to look it up after all. Aren't angels a combination of all the above? Turns out I knew all along.

Astrid's 78th Birthday.

EPILOGUE

Over thirty years have passed since Astrid left us. Dominic remained a patient at the Veteran's Hospital in Holyoke, Massachusetts until he passed away at the age of eighty-three in November 1995. Astrid's friend DD moved to California with her daughter and lived to the age of eighty, until her death in November 2008.

Our two boys, Billy and Nick, are presently older than Cindy and I were during those fateful few years with Astrid. Only from that perspective, do we realize how young we were then. We just felt much older at the time.

Billy, at the time of this writing, is thirty-five and has a beautiful wife Angela and three wonderful children Lily, Bryn, and Nicky.

Nick, now thirty-two years old, graduated from Northeastern University, served in Iraq, and now works in Washington DC. Cindy and I are divorced; each of us remarried but have remained very close friends over the years. My wife Chiara and I live in the Town of Agawam, a twenty-minute drive from Chicopee.

Cindy and her husband Tom still live next to Astrid's old house, which has since been occupied by a few different families over the years.

All the remnants of the garden are long gone, covered by a flat manicured grass carpet. The row of lilacs and the worn wooden picket fence that Astrid and I conversed over so many times has been replaced by a six-foot stockade fence. The adjacent backyards, no longer visible from each other, maintain the ultimate privacy.

Despite all that has changed, every now and then Astrid gently finds a way to remind us of her presence. Before this book was published (in fact, it wasn't considered a "book" at all at the time), while still in rough draft, I had shared with only a few people. It was too personal and I had no intention of publishing. The purpose of writing it down was to share with close family members. We didn't want the story to fade as the years went by or disappear entirely after Cindy and I are no longer around to tell it.

I had become friendly with our travel agent, Marge, who had arranged many trips for my current job. Marge is a very special and caring person and we'd have frequent conversations beyond the topics of work and travel.

I had to get my truck serviced at the Toyota dealership in West Springfield, which was right around the corner from Marge's office at World Wide Travel. While I waited for the work to be done, I thought I'd walk over to see Marge about an upcoming trip. We visited for a while and after the truck was ready, I walked back and drove off in a hurry to get back to work.

While driving next to Marge's office, I heard a funny noise underneath the truck and assumed I ran over something. When the noise became worse, rather than turn left towards my office, I took a right back towards the dealership and the truck began to wobble. I had just made it back into the service center parking area and heard a grinding noise followed by a disturbing thud. I stepped outside to see that the right front tire had fallen off, and the full weight of the front end was resting on the bolts. The lug nuts had not been replaced after changing the tire. The manager came out to see what happened and apologized profusely. He said they'd repair the damage and gave me a rental car to use in the meantime.

Driving past Marge's office for the third time (fourth if you count my earlier walk), I called to tell her what happened.

"Oh, my goodness," she said. "You could have been on the highway! Imagine if you lost control?" She went through a few of the "what if's" and insisted I must have a guardian angel watching over me. Hmm . . . I immediately thought of Astrid. As the conversation went through the topic of angels I asked Marge if she'd like to read a little story. I hadn't worked on it or even looked at it for several months, but Marge's comments reminded me.

As crude a draft as it was, I felt comfortable with Marge reading it. Within a few days, Marge called to say she liked the story and asked if she could share with her sister Pat. I didn't know Pat but said sure. It's only her sister, and it won't go anywhere beyond that anyway, so why not?

Marge later called to tell me that her sister Pat enjoyed reading it and asked if it would be ok to share with a few people at her church. My first reaction (which I kept to myself) was "no way" because I would then be getting into a "public" exposure that I wasn't ready for. It was one thing to share with close friends and family members but something entirely different with people I didn't know.

I suddenly became uncomfortable, and besides, it wasn't even finished. Marge suggested that I might want to go to the church myself; after all, if the story was to be shared why not from the person who wrote it? *Ok, Marge, don't get too carried away here,* I thought. I was starting to get nervous, but after further consideration, I became curious how people might react.

Before agreeing to anything, I had a few obvious questions, like, *where did Pat live and where is the church? What kind of church is it? How many people potentially was she thinking of sharing with?*

I was self-conscious and apprehensive about the exposure of such a personal experience. Also, I was a little afraid it wouldn't be interesting enough for strangers.

When Marge called back, she said that she wasn't sure of some details, but she knew Pat was a member of a small community church in Chicopee. She said she only wanted to share with a few people who might appreciate it.

A small community church in Chicopee, I wondered . . . *could it be?* Chances were too slim. St. Christopher's church, where Astrid, Cindy, and I had attended so long ago, was a small wooden A-framed church tucked away in a neighborhood, almost hidden, where not many people even knew it existed. It had been well over twenty years since the last time I had even laid eyes upon St. Christopher's church. I shrugged off the idea because it just seemed too unlikely.

Later that day, Pat confirmed, it was indeed the same St. Christopher's church. My first thought was, *Astrid was at it again – what other church could it have possibly been?* Of all the cities and towns, and the hundreds of churches in the area, what were the odds? The congregation of St. Christopher's consists of a mere forty families.

By the time I called Pat, she had shared the story with a few of her fellow parishioners, who just happened to remember Astrid, Cindy, and me. *After twenty-five years?* I was shocked. When Pat mentioned the names of people I remembered, so many memories came back. I just knew I had to pay a visit.

It was wonderful to see old acquaintances, and make new friends. Bill and Shirley Twining, Dan and Linda Paquette, Pam Bradshaw, and Dixie and Marcel Lauzon were people I remembered the most and there they were, like no time had passed. A few stories of Astrid were shared, and I was transplanted back in time, with old memories being resurrected. With the exception of just a few small renovations, the church had remained remarkably unchanged. It was very much like going back to an old comfortable home.

The only new aspect of visiting St. Christopher's was meeting The Rev. Scott Seabury. At the time, Father Scott had been at St. Christopher's for 10 years. Of course, he'd never had the opportunity to meet Astrid, but took a great interest in who she was, her story, and her impact on the church and community. I had an inkling, just one of those back of the brain hunches, that Father Scott would somehow be instrumental in perpetuating Astrid's legacy. In the months and years that followed, that proved to be true in many unexpected ways that continue through today.

I'm sure Astrid would be smiling if she can see how her act of kindness has spread all these years later – and right from St. Christopher's church! Sharing the story about Astrid with the right person at the right time unexpectedly brought it back full circle, to where it all began, so many years ago. I cannot think of a better way to say thank you to Astrid, except to give back, and of course, to fulfill an old promise. I wondered if my tire falling off at that particular moment was just another one of Astrid's ingenious little tricks. I can see her looking down, smiling through her window from heaven, once again amused at her ability to surprise us. Anything is possible, no explanation necessary.

*Cindy (Luba Hansen) and Mike (Jeremy Gladen) discuss
their future and getting a new car.*

LETTERS

The following are examples of letters received following the initial publishing of the book, showing how Astrid touched the lives of people in her community. To maintain privacy, names and personal information have been withheld.

August 2012

Dear Michael,

I was very surprised to see the article in the paper a few weeks ago. I had to read it a few times as I just couldn't believe it was about our friend Astrid who passed away so long ago. Well, that led me to buy the book because I had to read the WHOLE story. So much of your story sounded familiar — and confirmed what we suspected long ago.

In the late 70's, my husband lost his job and we were going through a rough time. Astrid offered to help but we politely declined. Next thing you know, a handful of our bills are paid — anonymously. She never admitted it, but we knew, and I think she knew we knew!

Astrid was like family to us, yet there was a lot about her that we didn't know. Thanks for sharing your story with us and shedding some light on the mystery!

Yours truly,

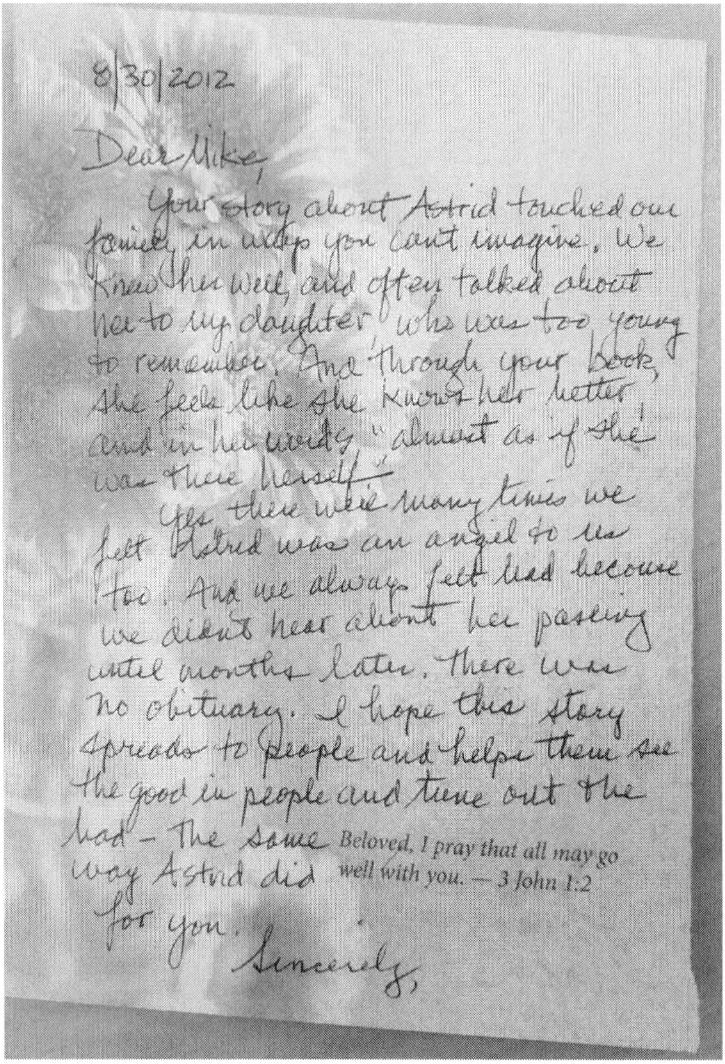

8/30/2012

Dear Mike,

Your story about Astrid touched our family in ways you can't imagine. We knew her well, and often talked about her to my daughter who was too young to remember. And through your book, she feels like she knows her better, and in her words "almost as if she was there herself."

Yes there were many times we felt Astrid was an angel to us too. And we always felt bad because we didn't hear about her passing until months later. There was no obituary. I hope this story spreads to people and helps them see the good in people and tune out the bad — The same way Astrid did for you.

Beloved, I pray that all may go well with you. — 3 John 1:2

Sincerely,

92

Sept 22, 2012

Hello Mike,

Just a quick note to say I enjoyed your book about Astrid. I knew Astrid and D.D. too, from the bakery we all worked at in Chicopee in the early 70's. She was a special woman and I can picture everything you described. And I believe it!! She was always there to help and had a habit of showing up at just the right times.

Thank you for bringing back cherished memories. It brought both tears and smiles!

Blessings

93

Mike

My name is Russell ████████, I have read the article in the Chicopee-Plus several times, I have yet to read your book..I can't believe how close to home this has come. My wife and I had become very close to Astrid and Domonic about the same period of time that you did. We also benifited from her generousity and were there to help them in any way we could. We were with her on that friday she was in the hospital we were going away for a couple of days. When we returned on Sunday I went to the hospital to visit only to find an empty room and that she had passed. I was heartbroken.

CAST AND CREW INTERVIEWS

Jason Campbell, the film's Producer, addresses a crowd prior to filming a scene at the Bridgeport United Methodist Church.

Jason Campbell – *Producer*

So, I get this phone call from a Christian book publisher in Massachusetts that represents several authors that wished to turn their books into films. Yes, of course I'm interested. They sent me the books and I planned a visit to meet with the authors in early Spring 2018. One of the authors was Mike Tourville, the writer of A PROMISE TO ASTRID.

On the one-hour flight to Boston, I knocked out Tourville's book. I loved it. I mean I really loved it; the story held my attention and that's really difficult to do. But what intrigued me most was why was Tourville releasing a book now on events that happened in his life thirty years ago?

The answer was quick to come after Mike took me to Astrid's house on Westover Road in Chicopee. As described so prolifically in his book, I felt I was there. I could see her gardens, I could see her looking over the fence in the backyard and snooping around the Tourville home.

I could see little Nick and Billy playing in the yard. The home was perfect for that young couple starting a family. Then, like magic it hit me standing in Astrid's backyard. I too had people like Astrid in my life; those that cared for me, helped me and guided me. I reflected back, and then I got it. That evening Mike and I planned the film A PROMISE TO ASTRID with a goal to make the story so authentic that it challenged audiences with a mandate to make kindness contagious.

We chose Bridgeport, WV as the film's home because the tremendous kindness shown from the community just matched the film's message. With the help from so many from this great community, Astrid the film came to life in four short months.

Oh, I could thank so many. But I would like to say 'thank you' to Mike Tourville and Cindy Mennard for bringing Astrid back to life and sharing her with all of us. Thank you for showing us her unique perspective in carrying one another's burdens. And most of all, thank you for challenging each of us in making compassion and kindness contagious.

JoAnn Peterson stars as Astrid Nicosia.

JoAnn Peterson – *"Astrid Nicosia"*

Last July I received a call from Jason Campbell, whom I'd never heard of, telling me I'd been recommended by Gary Vincent for a role in a movie that he was producing. That surprised me as I had only one line in a film Gary and I did together. But I am forever grateful that one line led to the Astrid role! When Gary sent me the script, I knew right away I wanted to play Astrid.

When Jason called and asked me to do a video audition, he described Astrid as a cross between Mary Poppins and Queen Elizabeth. So, the first thing I did was watch Mary Poppins! Many years ago, my Grandma Smith had given me some dresses from the '50s and '60s, in case I ever needed them for one of my stage roles, and they turned out to be perfect for the Astrid character! I memorized the side script, donned one of Grandma Smith's old dresses, took off my makeup, and added wrinkles and age spots. My husband Tom videotaped a garden scene in my backyard. Within 15 minutes of receiving the video, Jason called to offer me the role.

Once I read the book, I realized how blessed I was to be offered the role. It's a wonderful true story about an amazing woman. So many things came together, I feel God had a hand in giving me the role. I have a collection of angels; Astrid in our movie, collected angels. I found my late mom's Bible cover with angels on it and used it in the movie. My undergrad degree is in horticulture; Astrid loved her beautiful flower garden. I have a deep and abiding faith, believing God put me here to help others as did Astrid.

I asked my church and friends to pray for me because I was afraid I wouldn't be able to memorize all those lines. My friend G'na Stephens said, "If God calls you, he'll equip you. And God has called you." I felt her and many other's prayers.

When Dominic's role became open, Jason offered the role to my husband Tom, hoping we would have a natural rapport. It was wonderful sharing the experience with my husband! I could easily imagine how I would feel if anything ever happened to him. Acting like I love him was easy! I also appreciated having a few of my friends in roles (Denise

Myers) and as extras (Fred Conley, Dave Stephens, Brittany Warnick, Janet and Rick Turner). The cast and crew were so supportive and friendly. Brad, Danny, and Gary included me in discussions about how scenes could be shot and sometimes went with my idea, making me feel valued as an actor and a pro. Since Jeremy and I shared many scenes, I got to know him best. He's a very nice young man and a great actor.

I awoke one morning with the song *Angels Watchin' Over Me* going through my head. Jason agreed to add the song and I crooned it to Dominic to calm him and sang it with the choir (as myself) during Astrid's funeral! How many people can say they've attended and sang at their own funeral?

Jason also liked a quote I suggested: "I shall pass this way but once. Any good therefore that I can do or any kindness that I can show, let me do it now," which I used under my senior picture in my HS yearbook. Dean recited it in Pastor Seabury's sermon.

The hardest scene for me was the hospital bed scene. In the wig and makeup, I looked like my mom. My mom was in a hospital bed when she died only a year before. As the scene began, I could feel her presence and the grief of losing her came right back to me. When Jeremy leaned over me to hear my whispered words, my mother's last words came out of my mouth – "I love you all." I began sobbing. They had to stop filming while I composed myself to continue.

Most people are familiar with WWJD, meaning "What would Jesus do?" Now, when I encounter situations, I think WWAD? – "What would Astrid do?" She was an amazing woman. I am honored to have played her. I strive to be like her.

Michael Tourville (yes, "Michael") and I had talked for hours about what Astrid was like. He put me in contact with people who knew Astrid. I vividly recall Astrid's minister saying, "As a minister, I'm always giving, but with Astrid, I was on the receiving end."

I am so grateful to Jason Campbell for taking a chance on me and to Gary for recommending me for the role. And, how many actors can say they met the real people who were depicted in their movie? It was such a thrill to meet Michael, Cindy, their boys and Pastor Seabury. Wow! Just incredible! This entire experience was one I never thought I'd have.

For the last 11 years, JoAnn has performed living history first person portrayals, which she calls "Amazing Women of History", portraying Jenny Lind, Mary Lincoln, Margaret "The Unsinkable Molly Brown", Nellie Bly and Shirley Temple Black. Professional regional theater credits include Mother Abbess in "The Sound of Music", Mrs. Einsford-Hill in "My Fair Lady", Shandel in "Fiddler on the Roof", Mrs. Darling in "Peter Pan" (West Virginia Public Theatre); and Doris MacAfee in "Bye, Bye Birdie" (Cumberland Theatre). JoAnn has written eight murder mystery plays, and a Civil War show.

Jeremy Gladen stars as Mike Tourville.

Jeremy Gladen – *"Mike Tourville"*

I'm in a Facebook group, run by a friend of mine who posts auditions. I saw it and emailed a head shot and resume to Jason Campbell at JC Films. He quickly replied, asking for a reel. I directed Jason to my website, and he said he'd review with Mike Tourville and a few others to see if they thought he was a good fit. And the next day Jason offered me the part!

This was different than anything I've ever done; not just in terms of being one of the lead roles, but also the subject matter – being family-oriented, uplifting – that sort of thing. After reading the script, I took an immediate liking to Astrid's pay-it-forward character. It's influential through time – the endless giving back.

I was interested in not only the story itself, but it being based on a book of real human experience which, for an actor, is fun to explore. In every good story there is always something a character desires, something they need or want. I related to Michael's desire for happiness, to be able to balance his home life with his work life, to be in a place financially that would give him this ability and security, most importantly for his family. In finding this, the way we treat others is only a reflection of ourselves and it must come from within. Michael isn't blind to the things around him, love, family, friendship, etc., but he seeks a balance. Not to have it all, but enough. Through the difficulties and doubts I think by the end he finds the happiness he sought within and without...and, well, with a little help from Astrid, who is basically an angel. Yeah, that's what interested me.

Aside from the characters status, the material things, etc. being different from other roles I've played, similarly, Michael is determined. I like to work with similarities in myself with a character, he doesn't give up, which I've played in other roles. He's also not just determined for himself, but those around him. If he succeeds, his family succeeds, and who doesn't want that? It can be challenging, the stakes higher, but challenges are fun. I love a good challenge.

This was my first time working with the cast and crew. It wasn't until after production I realized Solon Tsangaras

103

(actor who plays Tim) and I worked on the same horror film back in 2006. Not together, but we both had roles.

I'm so humbled by the entire experience. The cast and crew were some of the best I've worked with. Dedicated and passionate, and with a good dose of humor. The entire city of Bridgeport opened their arms for all of us, many of them crew members, and were all so welcoming - great to see and very thankful for that.

The support of the community behind this film and the others JCFilms puts out is incredible, and to have been a part of that was an experience I'll never forget. That and the number sixteen, my favorite number of the bunch, found itself all over this script and in dates and times during the making. Call it what you want, but I took it as a sign that only good is happening around this project and it's something I should do.

I think this story teaches resilience above anything. No matter how big or small the difficulties in life can be we always find ourselves bouncing back, or at least the possibility is there if we're willing to accept. We're not all fortunate enough to have a neighbor like Astrid, but we realize, at the end of this story, the impact she has left on the community is one that exists beyond the tangible - that it is found within you, right in front of you.

Jeremy Gladen has lived and worked in LA for ten years. Most recently he played a supporting role in the upcoming thriller I SEE YOU (2019) starring Helen Hunt, directed by Adam Randall. He has worked on several feature and independent projects, short films, commercials, theatre, and behind the scenes. He had the pleasure of working with Christopher Nolan and his team as a post-production assistant on INTERSTELLAR (2014).

Astrid and Mike reflect on how he first met Cindy.

Luba Hansen as Cindy Tourville.

Luba Hansen – *"Cindy Tourville"*

Last summer, Brad Twigg texted me and asked if he could recommend me for a lead role in a movie with Dean Cain called A PROMISE TO ASTRID. Since I always have so much fun working with Brad I instantly said "Yes!" About a week later, Jason Campbell emailed me and asked to see my film reel. I emailed him back right away with my reel and acting resume.

After Brad told me about the movie, I started doing the research online. I learned that the movie was based on a book of the same name and it was based on a true story. My character, Cindy, was based on an actual person who was still living. I was so fascinated by my role that I couldn't wait to learn as much as possible about Cindy.

I read the book twice, highlighting any facts about Cindy that I needed to know, such as her emotions, and experiences about her husband Mike, and her boys. The BEST part was talking on the phone to the actual Cindy! It was so amazing to hear her voice. That day, I learned so much about my character. I read the script three times and each time I discovered something new about my character.

This role was very different than any other roles that I've played. A lot of the work I've done is with horror films or theater, but this my first role where my character was still living. I got to meet Cindy in person and that made it easier for me to portray the character.

I've worked with Brad, Gary and Daniel before for the Fuzzy Monkey Films (Brad's Production Company) for few years. Brad does horror films with lots of blood and gore which is the opposite of A PROMISE TO ASTRID. This was my first time working with Jason.

This was a great team of people that I loved working with, and I hope to continue creating amazing things with them. Jason is a director/producer who leaves the actor in his/her element. Jason was very flexible with the decisions that I made for my character and had faith in me to deliver the message that he was looking for in the film.

I grew up living and working in the big cities like Washington DC, and in the heart of Manhattan. Filming in a small town of Bridgeport where everyone knew each other was very interesting. There was a time when I went to get some coffee at Almost Heaven Desserts & Coffee Shop and a lady in line behind me asked me if I was one of the actresses in the movie with Dean Cain. She was so fascinated about the movie and how it was to be an actor. She even asked for my autograph. I told her that she was very sweet, but I was just a working actor and not famous at all. I learned a lot about Bridgeport! Now, I get really excited when I get a chance to go to a small town that I've never been to, because I know that I will come back having learned something new.

I probably would have never read A PROMISE TO ASTRID if Brad didn't recommend me because I've never read a faith-based novel before. It was a heartwarming story. I now recommend the book to all my friends and family when I talk about the movie. And the movie challenged me to be a better actor and expand my acting genre. I hope not to lose touch with everyone that I met through the film. I feel like I've made so many new friends!

Luba was born in Tula, Russia and lived in an orphanage until she was adopted at age 10 by an American family. From the age of 12 Luba began acting in local plays and auditioned as much as possible. After graduating from college, Luba worked for the Department of Agriculture (USDA) as a contractor which gave her enough flexibility to audition and model. While studying film and the Meisner technique at the New York Conservatory for Dramatic Arts in Manhattan, NY, Luba made extra money by doing small acting gigs and Off-Broadway plays. Moving back to the DC area in January of 2018, along with her childhood friend, Luba began a meal prep company called Healthy Fresh Meals, which prepares and delivers 1,500-2,000 meals per week.

Cindy and Mike share a tender moment.

Dean Cain stars as Pastor Scott Seabury.

"Michael Tourville's A PROMISE TO ASTRID is such a wonderful story of kindness and compassion. I'm so grateful to have been asked to be a part of this film and to actually meet many of the real people portrayed in the movie. It was a memorable experience!"

—Dean Cain

Michael Sigler stars as Russell Reynolds.

Michael Sigler – *"Russell Reynolds"*

I had already made several movies with Jason Campbell and he called to tell me about this story. It sounded interesting and he thought I'd be right for the character of Russell.

I read an early draft of the script and, no surprise, fell in love with it – especially with Astrid. I love the idea of redemption. Of course, as a Christian I have experienced forgiveness and redemption in my own life. Jesus paid for all my second (and third and fourth) chances. The story of Astrid parallels that in a way. I love that Russell became involved with Astrid's work. He was her co-conspirator. And the fact that Astrid was a woman made me think of my mom, who was so patient and forgiving of my missteps in my younger years.

Well, to my knowledge, this is the first time I've played a living person. I usually play characters in a position of authority: lawyers, bosses, businessmen, etc. It was a nice change to play a character that has been given a new outlook on life and is grateful for that gift. He's so grateful, in fact, that he begins using his skills to help his benefactor change the lives of others. It was a pleasure to play Russell because, as I said before, we as Christians have all been given a gift that we don't deserve, and I think that somewhere down inside we all feel the desire to pay it forward. And it feels so good when you do!

Jason is a great friend who has been there for me since we first met. I'll work with Jason until he can't stand looking at me anymore. :) Gary and I are relatively new friends. We had a scene together in THE FOLLOWER and we were both in a film called LOOPHOLE, but we didn't have any scenes together. We're working together on two new JC Films projects right now, NOT FOR SALE and A CHILD OF A KING, and I suspect there are a few more in the pipeline. I had not met Brad or Dan before, but I thoroughly enjoyed the experience. I like their style and their passion for storytelling. I hope I get the chance to work with them again in the future. I suspect that I will.

I had a wonderful time working with this cast and crew! When you meet a group of people with whom you share the same passions, you can pretty much bet you're going to get along. Of course, when you're filming little things pop up just like any family. So many things can lead to a shortened temper or a frayed nerve. But film casts and crews operate very much by a process of attrition. Everyone you meet is so very nice because if they weren't, they wouldn't be asked back. When you're going to be spending long hours in close quarters when it's either too hot or too cold and everyone is trying to do the best job they can, you don't want to be around grumps or whiners or meanies. Honestly, film and TV people are the nicest people I know. And the cast and crew of ASTRID were certainly no different.

There were a lot of laughs during filming and a lot of hugs and selfies and tears when it was over. You get really close to your crew and cast mates on a shoot. The more sequestered you are the closer you get. The whole process and everything about it really is magical to me!

Every movie has a lasting effect in one way or another. This one has me thinking about angels. I believe in angels. They don't have to real angels necessarily. They can be the human kind like Astrid. Or like my wife. Or my mom. Those who were sent directly from God to serve a certain purpose or to fulfill a certain need. I think I may have met an angel once. A lady came figuratively out of nowhere, ministered to me and then left as mysteriously as she had appeared. She reminded me in no uncertain terms that I "can do all things through Christ who strengthens me." She was surely sent by God whether she was an angel or not. It's more involved than that, but it's another story for another time.

The meals were amazing! Barb Knicely (who is also our cast mate) and the folks at the Bridgeport Country Club did such a wonderful job with the catering! Oh, don't worry; we still had the requisite amounts of donuts and granola bars and a wide selection of Fritos corn chips. And since we were in West Virginia, there were plenty of pepperoni rolls! God truly smiled on us the day he created the pepperoni roll!

In addition to A PROMISE TO ASTRID, Michael has two films that he's very proud of, THE CABIN and THE FOLLOWER, headed for distribution in the near future, so look for all three of those! This spring he's very excited to be filming projects in Arizona and Ecuador, with a few others on tap for later this year. Michael recently moved from the East Coast to Los Angeles to continue his journey! You can follow him at MichaelSigler.com.

Gary Lee Vincent, the film's Director, also has a cameo appearance as Mr. Mason, the Hospital Administrator.

Gary Lee Vincent – *Director, "Mr. Mason"*

The project was brought to my attention by Jason Campbell. I had worked with Jason on three previous projects (LOOPHOLE, THE FOLLOWER, and MEGAN'S CHRISTMAS MIRACLE) and since I lived in the area, Jason thought that this film and overall message would be a good fit.

Jason offered me an opportunity to co-direct the film and look for ways to bring interesting aspects to the visual experience of the storyline. I considered it to be both an honor and a challenge and welcomed the opportunity to work with Jason again. I had previously done numerous films and TV projects as an actor or producer, but this was going to be my first opportunity to fully be involved with helping Jason co-direct a project of his.

As previously mentioned, I worked on three of Jason's other films, and I knew Brad and Dan from even before then. I was a producer on a couple of Brad's horror films and enjoyed working on several projects with him since then. Dan is excellent to work with and is often helping on Brad's projects, so it has always been somewhat of an 'extended family' working with these incredibly talented people. Brad and I are both from West Virginia, so it seems natural to collaborate on projects with each other, especially since we are geographically close to many of the filming locations.

As a Director, this was very different. I have worked on over 60 film and television projects, but most of them have been as an actor or producer. To direct a picture is quite a big responsibility and undertaking, and I tried my best to give it the attention and thoroughness the position required.

I also have a cameo in A PROMISE TO ASTRID as Mr. Mason, the financial director of a hospital who must break the bad news to a grieving lady that her husband's insurance is not covering his medical care and that there is not a whole lot more the hospital can do. As an actor, I have played different professional types and this felt natural, even though this particular part is probably the closest thing to a villain role in the context of the ASTRID movie.

I had a very positive experience with all the cast and crew. We worked very well together, which is saying something, as you don't always have that on the set. The shooting schedule was compressed and we had to buckle down and pull off a long series of 12-hour days. Although all of us were under pressure and tired, I believe we all made it through the experience and are proud of the work we accomplished.

I don't want to come off sounding too supernatural, but I got the feeling that this project was blessed. There were several times when the script had flat spots in it, and I wasn't sure how the actors would respond. It was during those times that we got a 'nudge' for something totally out of left field that really made the shoot better than we could have planned.

Let me give you an example: There is a scene where Astrid goes to a special needs home to meet with the director (Madison) to help her fund the completion of a construction project (some dorms the home was building). The script called for Astrid to show up, look at the plans and make a donation. However, we had shot a scene with a talented actress, Ruth, that had Down Syndrome the day before and that person was with the group of folks at the home on the Madison day. As Astrid was interviewing Madison about the plans, Ruth comes over and gives Astrid a hug, making the *connection* of why homes like Madison was running was so important. In other words, it went from a flat financial scene, to showing *who* was being helped and *why* helping others was so important.

The story of Astrid is a story about giving and helping others; it's a story of paying it forward. I think that we need stories like this from time to time to allow us to take our own lives into perspective and know that we all struggle and sometimes if we can help someone in some way ease their struggle, perhaps we should. You never know when you yourself may need help from someone and it sure is a blessing when that unexpected help arrives in just the right time.

I want to sincerely thank Jason Campbell and Mike Tourville for allowing me this opportunity to co-direct A PROMISE TO ASTRID. This project is very special, and it took a degree of trust in my abilities to help tell this incredible story. It is my sincere hope that the story of Astrid will touch many lives and give us all an opportunity to work together on a future endeavor.

Gary Lee Vincent was born in Clarksburg, West Virginia and is an accomplished actor, producer, author, musician, and entrepreneur. Gary has appeared in multiple plays and concerts throughout his life, but got his motion picture acting debut at the age of 40 in the horror movie BELLY TIMBER starring in the role of George Pogue, one of the founders of Indianapolis.

To date, he has starred in over sixty feature films, including MY UNCLE JOHN IS A ZOMBIE!, KILLER CAMPOUT, WRESTELMASSACRE, DEATH HOUSE, MY FRIEND DAHMER, SKB, BLACK PANTHER, THE KINGSBURY RUN, ABOVE SUSPICION, SOLVER, NIGHTBLADE, THE FINAL INTERVIEW, and many others.

In television, he has starred in MINDHUNTER (Season 1), HOUSE OF CARDS (Season 5), THE WALKING DEAD (Season 8), and Stranger Things (Seasons 2 and 3).

After directing A PROMISE TO ASTRID, Gary directed his second feature film, a comedy called DESK CLERK, in early 2019.

In 2010, his horror novel DARKENED HILLS was selected as 2010 Book of the Year winner by Foreword Reviews Magazine and became the pilot novel for a six-book series of vampire books called Darkened, which includes the novels DARKENED HILLS, DARKENED HOLLOWS, DARKENED WATERS, DARKENED SOULS, DARKENED MINDS, and DARKENED DESTINIES. For more information, visit www.garyvincent.com.

Brad Twigg (right), the film's Director of Photography, sets up a camera for a funeral home scene. Brad also stars as the Hospital Receptionist.

Brad Twigg – *Director of Photography, "Hospital Receptionist"*

Gary Vincent contacted me to see if I'd be interested in being the cinematographer for this new film he was co-directing. I knew nothing about it before then. I've worked as a cinematographer on many films in the past, but this was the first of this genre. It was definitely a new experience. I love to be creative and try to take advantage of any opportunity that allows me to do so. This project seemed different and offered a new creative challenge.

I've had the honor of working with Gary, Dan Brooks, Luba Hansen and Richie Acevedo on multiple occasions and was very happy to have them involved with the film.

Behind the scenes, Gary and Dan are both hard workers and bring a lot of creativity to the table. They all do amazing work and are wonderful to work with.

The rest of the cast, many of whom I'd never met before, was extremely professional, great to work with, and a lot of fun. Everyone got along great – it was actually disappointing when it was over!

There were so many interesting experiences on set, it would warrant a book of its own. While most of my projects are fictional stories, what was unique about this film is that it was a true story, and we were portraying real people. A few of them, Mike, Cindy, and Scott Seabury were actually present for some of the filming.

The movie allowed me to meet lots of wonderful people, and also broaden my experience into a new film genre. I hope viewers enjoy this film. It's a beautiful story and shouldn't be missed!

Brad Twigg is a producer and director, known for FRAMES OF FEAR (2016), KILLER CAMPOUT (2017) BRUTALITY (2018), WRESTLEMASSACRE (2018), and HARVEST OF HORRORS (2019).

Production Assistant Daniel Brooks, is pictured here configuring the sound and lighting for a large church scene.

Daniel Brooks – *Production Assistant*

I've worked on many projects with Brad Twigg as an "everything" guy (sound/lighting/FX/actor...etc.) He asked if I could join the crew for this film and I was excited as always to be a part of the team!

When on a set like this I'm always fascinated to meet two personalities from each individual. To explain, every actor was so believable that when "action" was called I got to "meet" a whole other group of real, and real interesting, people... not just "characters". The first time seeing Astrid (JoAnn Peterson) out of character was, I think, on day 3... and many of us thought *"Who is this new lady on set?"* And then, adding to that, was meeting the "real" Mike, Cindy, and Scott Seabury. It just multiplies!

I've had the pleasure of sharing the set on previous movie projects, both behind and in front of the camera with Gary, Luba, Richie and Jessie. And I must mention that all my film experience has had Brad Twigg right there teaching me the ropes hands on. This was the first time (but hopefully not the last time) working with Jason as he was great to work with!

Sets can be stressful at times (except for me because I'm just that easy going) but the set crew/cast meshed so well it was like working with close friends even though most of us just met for the first time.

My full-time job occupies most of my time, so most of the projects I'm involved with are during weekends or days off. A PROMISE TO ASTRID was nearly continuous from day one "action" to "that's a wrap". And I enjoyed every day of it!

This film has definitely made an impact on me... Astrid's willingness to work with people when they are going through a rough time helps me to have patience with those who are not at their best time of their life when I meet them. It really makes you think more about it.

Daniel Brooks is known for his work on DEATHBOARD (2019), THEATRE OF THE DERANGED III and HARVEST OF HORRORS (2019).

Phuong Kubacki stars as Madison.

Phuong Kubacki – "Madison"

I found out about the movie when I saw a casting notice for it online in August of 2018. I submitted my headshot and reel and was booked!! When I got the script, I couldn't stop reading it. I finished it in one sitting. What interested me in the movie and role was that it was such an inspirational story that just promoted helping each other and having faith.

I was cast as the role of "Madison" who managed a home for people with special needs. Astrid stepped in and helped her achieve some of her goals to help more people. I've never played a role like this before. She was on a mission to execute such a great plan and eventually did. Hopefully I get to play more parts like this!

This was my first experience working with all of them, but my experience working with everyone was truly amazing! Everyone was so kind and helpful. I just got cast as a lead in their upcoming feature "John Light" to be filmed in Phoenix, AZ starring Dean Cain. I had one scene with Dean and he was so nice and such a pleasure to work with. All the other actors were also great and very talented. I look forward to working many more films with this cast and crew in the future.

The movie/book has definitely put a spotlight on faith-based films for me. I love the positive messages they send and feel great about the work being done.

In addition to the two movies she is filming with JC Films, Phuong Kubacki stays very busy acting on other projects. In 2018, she wrapped on the Lifetime film DYING FOR A BABY and MAX RELOAD and the NETHERBLASTER. She has also been featured on the Conan O'Brien Show, and you can currently watch her on Amazon Prime in the tv show THAT 80's GUY and feature film DUEL AT THE MOUND. When she is not filming, she is also a professional photographer and model. For more updates, follow her on instagram at @phuongtourage and on IMDB at imdb.me/phuong .

Katherine Shaw stars as diner waitress Tiffany.

Katherine Shaw – *"Tiffany"*

I had just completed a film MEGAN'S CHRISTMAS MIRACLE with Jason Campbell and he excitedly told me about a new movie he was making! I loved the Pay it Forward theme. It's a feel-good movie with heart, humor, and warmth.

I worked with Jason on Megan's Christmas Miracle. First time with Gary, Brad, and Dan. I loved working with this crew. They were super easy to work with, kind, and professional.

I always like to watch fellow actors. I learn so much from them. It's fun to watch the crew work and piece moments and beats and scenes together. This whole group felt like a family. Whenever I work with Jason, it seems to feel that way.

Makes you think more about ways you can help people around you. Also makes you think if maybe some of the people around you, aren't really angels. This was my favorite part about the movie. Angels among us.

Katherine Shaw studied Film and Theater at the University of Kansas and has danced and cheered for the NFL (Rams) and was a DJ at the top of Airthrey Castle in Scotland with her own radio show. She is an actress known for MEGAN'S CHRISTMAS MIRACLE (2018), a certified scuba diver and yoga instructor, and owns her own destination wedding and event company, www.CallaEventTravel.com.

Susanne Neff stars as Caroline.

Suzanne Neff – *"Caroline"*

I first noticed the title when I was inquiring about the movie. I then researched the story and saw it was a book. This prompted me to order a copy and read it. I played the role of a women that was in a desperate situation because of her husband's health and mounting hospital bills. I have played similar roles; a parent in despair, wife that feels hopeless, very similar emotions.

It was my first time working with JC films and it was a great experience. Jason is not only professional but also easy to work with. I always love getting to know other actors/crew in this industry. It was also pretty neat we were able to meet the author, and other "real" people from the book!

I love this story...this *true story* of how giving, attentive, and influential this woman was to so many around her. It challenges and inspires me. There are individuals all around us that need help. We are the hands and feet of God and I think we often get so caught up in our everyday lives we forget about those around us. She didn't allow distractions, she noticed, and listened to the Holy Spirit and didn't hesitate.

Suzanne grew up singing and performing from a young age in her native Jacksonville, Florida. She studied Theater and Communication Studies in college and performed in local theaters while moving around the country with her military family. Since moving to Northern Virginia, she has acted in short and feature films, national TV series, industrials and local commercials. Some of her recent projects are feature film FIRST LADY starring Nancy Stafford, coming summer 2019, and a feature film and ongoing web series MOUNT HIDEAWAY MYSTERIES available on Amazon. Suzanne is also known for FOR THE GLORY (2012), TOUCHED BY GRACE (2014) and AFTER SCHOOL (2016). She loves spending time with her family and teaching Communication Studies and doing voice over work for Northern Virginia Community College.

Heather Mudrick stars as Linda Seabury.

<u>Heather Mudrick</u> – *"Linda Seabury"*

What I loved most about A PROMISE TO ASTRID were all the people involved. I got personally involved early on just after the script was written and the search for all the locations started. As my home quickly became home base for the production, I quickly learned the amount of effort and hard work it takes to manage a film production. It was a blast for me and my family to participate.

As I mentioned, I became aware of the story early. I had read the book and even the script. I immediately became intrigued by this lady and in my head had imagined what she would look like. To watch Astrid come to life and see JoAnn Peterson portray her was everything I had imagined her to be.

Another portrayal I had the opportunity to witness first hand was the overall theme throughout the film–Kindness. From all the actors that travelled in, the crew that worked tirelessly and all the efforts of many volunteers I saw first-hand the underlining theme of this film in all of them: genuine kindness.

Thank you Mike Tourville and your family for sharing Astrid with me and my family and now the world.

Timothy E. Goodwin stars as Ronald.

Timothy E. Goodwin – *"Ronald"*

I've done about 12 films with Jason Campbell and he first told me about the project in the summer of 2018. Now, if someone offers me a role, I'll take a look before deciding, but with the trust I have with Jason and his group, I immediately said "Yes".

I play Caroline's husband Ronald, who is hospitalized for most of the film. In the end, we share our "story" with Astrid.

As a character actor, most of my roles are different than the others. I've played good guys, bad guys, confused guys —you name it, I'll play it! I was only on set for a day so I didn't get to know some of the cast and crew that well, but I can say the experience was fantastic. It's always a pleasure to work on a film and meet new people (and of course, see old friends).

Timothy E. Goodwin was born on November 13, 1968 in Bangor, Maine, as Timothy Earle Goodwin. He is an actor and producer, known for ADAM RUINS EVERYTHING (2015), WET HOT AMERICAN SUMMER (2015), and GILMORE GIRLS: A YEAR IN THE LIFE (2016). He has been married to Denise since 1992.

Becky Rosser stars as Heather.

Becky Rosser – *"Heather"*

I met Jason Campbell in the spring of 2018 at a Meet and Greet with Dean Cain when they were in town wrapping up a few scenes for Megan's Christmas Miracle. I helped him out with lodging in the area and he gave me tickets to the event with the promise that I could be an extra in a scene.

A few short months later Jason emailed and asked me if I would be interested in being cast. I didn't hesitate a second before shouting out, "Yes, of course!" even without knowing a thing about it. How ironic that Jason's promise to Becky was for a movie called A PROMISE TO ASTRD! I guess it was meant to be!

Being a part of a movie has been a lifelong dream of mine, so I was ecstatic to be offered a role. I never imagined it would come to life for me. Jason sent the script and I loved it! Then I read the book. I wanted to know everything about it that I could. When Jason asked me to play the Heather character in the movie and that he had me in mind when writing the script for that part, I couldn't believe it! I had no experience and he barely knew me but was willing to give me a chance.

I loved my character! It allowed me to be myself in a way. I could relate to her. The mentorship I felt Heather had with Astrid, I also have a person who has helped me through tough times I have had personally. I couldn't have chosen a better character for myself.

A PROMISE TO ASTRID was my first movie experience, and the first time ever working with any of the cast and crew. They are all absolutely amazing. Everyone was so down to earth, and genuinely wanted to help each other improve. I didn't know exactly what to expect going into this and was worried to pieces about messing up my lines or not doing something how they wanted me to. But Jason, Gary, and the other actors allowed you to be yourself, and I was grateful for their confidence in me. And since filming Astrid, I've had a few more opportunities to be involved more with more film projects.

This story makes you feel good and makes you want to be a better person. It makes me hopeful that there are truly good people in this world who simply want to do good and help others. There are so many people that you come across, and you judge them for whatever reason. You don't know what they are going through, or their story might be. Maybe they just need a smiling face, hope, and kindness. I want to be a person who makes an impact, much like Astrid did with so many people in her community.

It's interesting how I never knew Astrid or any of the other characters, but I felt a deep connection and emotionally attached to the characters. I will always be grateful for this experience.

Heather is surprised by a job offer from Astrid, while Dominic sleeps.

Professional wrestler Richie Acevedo plays Rocco, a junkyard owner about to give Mike a really hard time.

Richie Acevedo – "Rocco"

I really never heard of the book or movie until the cinematographer Brad Twigg asked me if I was interested on a role for the film. I have worked with Brad Twigg in several of his films including starring in WRESTELMASSACRE.

I took a quick look at the script and thought I fit the character perfectly! I'm glad Jason and Gary thought so too! I played Rocco and it seemed like an easy and fun role to play for me since I was a heel (bad guy) in Pro Wrestling. I've had a lot of practice playing bad guys. Being a Pro Wrestler/Sports Entertainer, I enjoy these kinds of projects. Life is full of new adventures!

I enjoyed working on this project, meeting new people, and hope to work with Jason Campbell on more projects.

Richie Acevedo (aka the Cuban Assassin) has been a professional wrestler since 1989 and turned to acting in 2013. Richie has appeared in several films such as LUNATIQUES - French Canadian TV series (1999), MILFs vs ZOMBIES (2015), BOUNTY HUNTER WAR (2014), THE MAKING OF THE MOB, New York (2015), and CONCUSSION (2015).

Veronica Rogers stars as Dominic's daughter, Robin.

Veronica Rogers – *"Robin"*

I heard about the movie from the website via Facebook. Jason had posted it and I responded to his post. I worked with Jason on three other films. Also worked with Dean, Tim Goodwin & Michael Sigler before. They are just wonderful people. So blessed to know them.

My first interest was that it was a faith-based movie, second was that it was based off a true story, third was that it was JCFilms doing the movie, forth, it was being shot in WV, and fifth, well, I thought I could put some feeling into the character I was portraying. Hopefully, it will come across to the audience as so. It was different simply because it was based on a true-life story. Other roles were fictional characters and this one had a better depth of meaning to me.

Everyone was helpful and Tim Goodwin was still his ever-encouraging self. Michael was just as funny as ever. Dean was still just as happy to have his picture made with strangers as he ever has been.

I drove 3 hours to do one scene, which took about 1 hour to shoot, then back into the car for another 3 hours to get home. That was interesting... but while we were there shooting, Jason was very kind and offered my husband to be an extra in a scene. My husband accepted, which made the long drive home seem not so long after all.

The great feeling of being a part of a film that has this kind of potential to impact folks with a simple but profound message of helping others is tremendous! This film will be TIMELESS! Its message will reach generations now and forever more with hope of how simple acts of kindness can effect positive change in the lives of others. I have no doubt that whoever sees this film, will afterwards walk away saying, *"That was a good movie!"*

Veronica Rogers is an actress, also known for THE FOLLOWER (2019), and MEGAN'S CHRISTMAS MIRACLE (2018).

Kathy Sanders stars as Angela.

Working on A PROMISE TO ASTRID was a truly magical experience!

I heard about the casting via a post on Facebook. When I read the synopsis and followed up with an internet search on the book, I knew I wanted to be a part of this beautiful project in any capacity!! I was so drawn to the story of Astrid's caring nature and her desire to be anonymous, yet she was very feisty and had a quick wit. I adored how the story brought to life the theme of simply caring for others. I've always believed that God places people in our lives at appointed times for an anointed purpose. Astrid's story shows that caring can come in many forms like lending a listening ear, giving a healing hug or purchasing a much-needed car.

After submitting, Jason contacted me stating that the role of Astrid had been cast and asked if I'd be interested in a small role... Would I?! YES! ANYTHING! I told him I'd get the coffee, scrub the floors, hold the lights, etc., whatever he needed! (And this statement holds true for any of his projects as I'm a huge fan!).

I adored my role as 'Angela', and although she was a fictional character in this movie version of the true story, her story had a beautiful arch. I found it very interesting that within this particular storyline, Astrid discovers she has inadvertently made a misstep and needs to recover.

I had worked with my dear friend Michael Sigler, who plays 'Russell', on many projects in DC so when I discovered that he was involved, naturally my enthusiasm increased tenfold!! (Truth be told, I did ask him to throw my name in the hat...hey, what can I say, I studied marketing and PR...).

One experience that impacted me greatly was filming in the homeless shelter. When the crew pulled in some of the residents to be in a few shots, their eyes lit up and you could see such joy in their sense of purpose and worth. I pray that they continue to feel that sense of worth forever.

The only way I can describe working with this amazing cast and crew on this beautiful project is MAGICAL and a true BLESSING! I remember being on set and thinking, "Is this really happening? I never want this to end. These people are amazing! Thank you GOD for this opportunity and my new film family! There was so much joy, laughter, creativity, respect, kindness, professionalism and just pure fun!! Lots and lots of fun!!

My final thought is a prayer:

I pray that this film blesses all who see it and I pray that it causes a tsunami of copycat kindness.

Kathy Sanders is an actress and producer, known for CHANCE WEB SERIES (2017) and THE FORGIVING.

A homeless Angela checks herself and her children into the mission.

Deborah Thompson stars as Russell Reynold's wife, Lynn.

Deborah Thompson – *"Lynn Reynolds"*

God winked at me and smiled. That sums up how I felt about being cast in A PROMISE TO ASTRID.

In another lifetime, as a very young woman and brand new Christian, singing and acting were my passions. An apprenticeship with the Pittsburgh Civic Light Opera was within my grasp. However, I just couldn't reconcile this pursuit with my new fledgling faith. Acting in a secular world created too much of an inner conflict for me. At that time, Christian theater and films were mostly unheard of. I chose to walk away and give my acting desire back to God.

Psychotherapy, my career and ministry became my passion for the next 30 years. Last year, however, found me soul weary, burnt out, and in need of something creative to restore me. "God, you know I thrive on creative outlets. They have all dried up. Could you just send me something, anything, just a quick breath of creative fresh air?"

He delighted me with an answer: A link to auditions for A PROMISE TO ASTRID, a film ALL about God sending hope and delight to tired people through the person of Astrid. (JoAnn Peterson embodied this special spirit perfectly with her portrayal.)

And so it was, at almost 60 years of age God gave my desire back to me, for just a brief moment in time, a momentary "breath of fresh air," so that I could once again return to my career and serve Him refreshed.

Barry Dailey stars as Dan, the car dealership manager.

Barry Dailey – "*Dan*"

I honestly had not heard of this story before my casting, but quickly came to appreciate and become inspired by the strength and impact she embodied, the power of God's reach through her. My role was a more genteel one for me, the second such role with a JCFilms production. I typically portray darker characters, so these have been a welcomed step into the shoes of kinder characters. Working with JCFilms and his crew has been a pleasure, from the process itself to the details Jason tends to himself, I am always made to feel a valuable part of the project and team. I look forward to working with Jason and his crew again soon.

Barry Michael Dailey is an actor known for CHOICES (2018), MEGAN'S CHRISTMAS MIRACLE (2018), and FOR THE GLORY (2012).

Dennis Marburger discusses a bad wreck in the road.

Dennis Marburger – *"Man in traffic jam"*

I submitted for the movie via email. I then received an email from Jason saying I was cast. He eventually called me to touch base and said that he was interested in my being involved with the movie because of the positive things he heard about me from Michael Sigler. It was a true pleasure meeting and working with Jason. I'm pretty sure it will be an ongoing relationship!

I was actually more interested in getting involved with the JC Films "family", then thinking about a specific role. It was a small speaking role (truck driver) with some dialogue with Jeremy Gladen (Mike Tourville, the lead). What made it different was the need to change some dialogue at the very last minute. The truck I was supposed to be driving never showed up, so we substituted my car. However, as we were ready to begin filming, I realized that some of my dialogue was connected to my being in a truck. I quickly thought of how I could change the dialogue to fit the new situation, and Jason approved.

I had previously known Michael Sigler and followed his work. While we had not actually worked together on the same project, we had mutual respect for each other's work and talent and had studied under the same acting coach. It was great to finally be on a set with him! I had shot on an award-winning web series with Kathy Sanders where I played her ex-husband. I also previously worked with Luba Hanson. This was my first time working with the JC Films crew.

It was a true pleasure to work with the cast & crew. Everyone was extremely outgoing, friendly, and supportive. It is like a true family group that I look forward to working with again & again! I drove 5 hours to set that day, and then since it took less time to shoot the scene than was scheduled, I drove 6 hours back home through torrential downpours. But it was all worth it to be a part of this project!

Dennis Marburger has been acting and singing since he was a child, and received a Theater degree in college. Dennis has performed in numerous theater organizations throughout his life with over 40 stage credits to his name. Nearly all were musicals, where he can use his baritone voice to enhance the roles. In August of 2016 he began doing on camera work and now works a full-time TV, Film, Commercial, Industrial, and Voice-Over career!

A wreck has traffic tied up for miles.

Donna Elsey stars as the Librarian.

Donna Elsey – *"Librarian"*

I met Jason Campbell a few years ago and became friends. One evening last summer I was at the Wonder Bar Steak House and Jason and Dean Cain were there filming a scene for Megan's Christmas Miracle. They needed extras and I volunteered. During that project Jason told me he was working on another movie and asked for my help. I helped get food donated for the crew and helped him find locations for A PROMISE TO ASTRID. He even gave me a small part with one line as a Librarian.

I had ordered the book A PROMISE TO ASTRID and enjoyed reading it. It was so interesting to watch this book come to life. The entire process was so interesting and fun, especially to see everything come together start to finish. I really enjoyed getting to know Gary Vincent, Brad Twigg, Michael Sigler and Solon Tsangaras. I found out that my youngest daughter is Gary's dentist!

I hope I was a help to Jason and the cast and crew and look forward to working with them again. I was so pleased to meet the real Mike and Cindy and also Rev. Seabury. It was a fantastic experience!!

Tom Peterson stars as Dominic.

Tom Peterson – *"Dominic"*

I came to be in A PROMISE TO ASTRID after my wife JoAnn was cast as Astrid. When the Dominic role became available, Jason asked if I'd be interested as I had quite a bit of stage experience, but this was my first movie role. I read the book to get a better feel for the character, and was really impressed by Astrid's and, by extension, Dominic's kindness, benevolence, and their pay-it-forward philosophy. I found I really liked these people and wish more folks were like them. Even though Dominic was having dementia problems, I loved the way he always magically appeared when Astrid needed him. Since Dominic was an Air Force veteran, I adlibbed a little experience into the movie.

I found the crew and rest of the cast very easy to work with and enjoyed their expertise and valued their suggestions and direction. And as always, with this shared experience, we met a lot of great people that we can call friends now.

Among other roles, Tom Peterson has played Harold Hill in THE MUSIC MAN, Father in CHILDREN OF EDEN, and Michael in I DO I DO. Tom also sang lead in a barbershop quartet for 20 plus years.

Barb Knicely stars as a Waitress and was the film's caterer.

Barb Knicely – "Waitress", catering meals for cast and crew

I read an article about it that Julie Perine wrote on *Connect Bridgeport*, where Jason Campbell had solicited help from the community for the movie. I manage the Bridgeport Country Club, and offered our conference room if they needed the facilities for rehearsals or for a cast party. He asked if I'd be willing to organize meals for the cast and crew while filming was taking place and I was happy to do that. The country club provided a lot of the meals, and several members helped by delivering to different set locations.

It was always fun to see bits and pieces of the filming, and sometimes becoming an impromptu extra, when I delivered food! It's going to be so cool to see it all come together in the movie! I feel like I've made friends for life through this experience.

I never imagined I'd have a part in the movie because I've always been a behind the scenes kind of person, but when Jason asked me, I was excited to do it. As I read over the script, I knew it was going to be a special movie with an important message. I've never played any other roles

Although my part was small, I spent a lot of time on the set providing meals for the cast and crew. Everything ran smoothly and everyone was so pleasant to be around. They were always encouraging and complimenting each other and offering assistance when needed. Everyone worked well together and truly felt like family!

It was heartwarming to see that people do genuinely care for others. It's refreshing to see people doing things to help and not want anything in return. It has made me keep my eyes open for ways to help people every day. It was truly an enjoyable experience for me both on the set and behind the scenes.

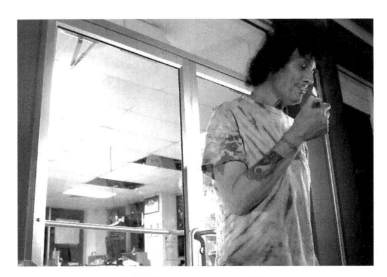

Solon Tsangaras stars as Tim.

Solon Tsangaras – *"Tim"*

From the moment I heard about this project from Jason Campbell, I knew something special was happening. He mentioned Gary Lee Vincent and Dan Brooks would be involved and I had worked with each of them on separate occasions. It was like hitting the trifecta. And then he said Michael Sigler, Luba Hansen, Tim Goodwin, and Richie Acevedo (who I had been in other movies with) had roles, I was thrilled to be reunited with them. A lot of serendipity going on here!

We discussed a few possible roles, which eventually led to playing Tim. I'm getting good at playing goofy homeless guys, and the Tim role fit right in. I was a homeless guy in THE FOLLOWER and had a brief appearance in MEGAN'S CHRISTMAS MIRACLE.

At least I didn't get killed in this movie! And I don't really mind being typecast – I'm happy to enhance the role with some genuine personality traits!

I've never seen myself acting outside my comfort zone in the horror genre, but I've done three faith-based films now. It's nice to play someone who starts out pretty nasty, but has some redemption and in the end the audience can shed a tear of happiness for him.

It was just wonderful working with this cast and crew! It was amazing to see the transformation from the acted roles to real life and back. Watching from "behind the scenes", there were moments the actors were so convincing they brought tears to our eyes. I remember saying *"You guys are good at this!"*

One of my observation in the ASTRID movie is that each of the characters are challenged and go through changes. But Astrid remains consistent and *persistent* throughout the movie. Each of the characters are pulled up by Astrid, and each rises above their adversity.

This movie was a unique experience, and a glaring example of the whole being greater than the sum of its parts. Everyone had a positive attitude, harmonious interactions, and a lot of new friendships were made. The final movie is a reflection of all of that.

Solon Tsangaras was born and raised in Queens, N.Y., performing in stage productions and video shorts and commercials as well as being involved with many bands throughout the 70's and 80's. He majored in Theater Arts, English and Communications. In the late 80's, he began a 20 year involvement with one of Long Island's top bands, Uncle Fester. He now lives in a quiet little village in Upstate New York with his lovely girlfriend Stephanie and their 8 feline 'kids', and continues to work in the acting and music fields, as well as writing novels and screenplays.

Solon's novels include: DETOUR TO ARMAGEDDON, BELLY TIMBER, and ATTACK OF THE MELONEADS. Solon's acting credits include MY UNCLE JOHN IS A ZOMBIE!, KILLER CAMPOUT, HER NAME IS CHRISTA, and A PROMISE TO ASTIRD. Solon's music credits include SOFA KINGDOM and the soundtrack for MY UNCLE JOHN IS A ZOMBIE!

Astrid attends a church service with Mike and Tim.

Cathy Jones stars as Ruth.

Cathy Jones – *"Ruth"*

Written by Carmen Jones, Cathy's Mom

I was told by Stepping Stones that Jason Campbell was making a new movie. He had most of it planned out, but didn't know what to do for one part of the book A PROMISE TO ASTRID, that it is based on. The story line was about a special need's person. Jason had little or no experience with special needs people, but one day he was eating lunch at Wendy's, he saw Cathy cleaning trays, tables and chairs. A light bulb went on! He was inspired to ask Cathy to be in the movie.

This was Cathy's first movie! She *loves* movies. She has about every Disney super Hero, Scooby Doo, or other PG movie you can name. What does she spend her hard-earned money on – movies! So, when she was asked if she wanted to be *in* a movie, she was *so excited*!!

When Jason opened the filming session at DJ's Diner with a prayer, I knew we had made the right decision to let Cathy be in the movie. I absolutely *loved* seeing Jason, this tall guy, climb under a small diner table to knock trays off for Cathy. Jason was trying to tell Cathy to "accidently" knock off the trays she would be cleaning. Cathy never drops trays at her real job, so, as her Mom, I saw her frustration or confusion as to what Jason was asking. I told her, "Cathy, I know you don't drop trays at work, but this is pretend. Can you pretend to knock trays off the table?" Jason must have overheard our conversation because seconds later he was asking for some kind of tape. He put one end of the duct tape on the bottom of a tray and sat it on the table. Then he had Cathy put the trays she cleaned on top of that one. He then somehow proceeded to pull on the other end of the tape, making the trays fall off the table. That showed Jason's true character to me!

Cathy wanted to give Jason a hug after that session. She asked me to take a picture and I got my phone out. She had Jason kneel down on one knee to be at her level. With her two fingers, she gave him a "rabbit ears" for the picture. She does that for people she likes to tease. Jason said, "Did you just give me rabbit ears?" Then he told me, as he pointed to me smiling, "I want a copy of that!"

Love, love, love, this story about Astrid! It has instilled a determination to love those around us more and to help those less fortunate than we are. Cathy and Astrid are two peas in a pod. Cathy helps others everywhere she goes!

A group photograph taken while filming scenes at Stepping Stones in Morgantown, WV.

Cindy Pulice stars as Paige, Ruth's Mom.

Cindy Pulice – *"Paige", Ruth's Mom*

In the spring of 2018, Jason Campbell contacted me at the Studio 9 Dance Academy in Bridgeport. He was interested in filming a movie, MEGAN'S CHRISTMAS MIRACLE at the studio. I had to inform Jason I was the previous owner of the dance studio, formerly known as Annabel Timms School of Ballet. I referred him to the new owner, Heather Mudrick. Next thing you know, we're filming a movie! It was at this time Jason informed us of his plans for a new movie, A PROMISE TO ASTRID.

As arrangements were made over the summer of 2018, my daughter Chiara auditioned for a role and was offered a small part. She immediately said yes! So I just sent my resume in as an afterthought to help her prepare her audition tape. And then I got a part also. It was such a wonderful experience to rehearse with her and watch her work so professionally with the cast and crew. I am so proud of her!

This was so exciting but also frightening at the same time! I've done many stage roles but never on film. This was a completely different experience - a lot more goes into it than I ever expected. Having 300 people watching from an audience is a completely different experience than having a camera right in front of your face!

It's great to see the buzz around town, the community involvement, and the uplifting message the film conveys. The camaraderie among the cast and crew was fantastic, and we made so many new friends. I feel blessed to be a part of it all, especially to share it with my daughter Chiara.

Chiara Pulice stars as the Nurse at Station.

Chiara Pulice – *Nurse at Station*

It was such an honor to have a role in A PROMISE TO ASTRID. Although I grew up doing musical theatre, this was my first movie! The last time I had to memorize lines was in 2013 when I played Elle Woods in "Legally Blonde The Musical!" The fact that I had a performance opportunity in my hometown (Bridgeport, WV) was just so awesome!

In 2019, I will graduate with a Master's in Integrated Marketing Communications! I currently live in Nashville, Tennessee and I intern at Sony Music! In undergrad, I was a member of the West Virginia University Dance Team! I absolutely love the arts, and I am interested in a career in the entertainment industry! Being a part of this movie confirmed that I want to have a career in entertainment, whether I am the one performing, or behind-the-scenes!

I really love what Jason is doing, and I'm so excited to see what the future holds for JC Films! Participating in this movie has been an inspiration for many reasons. I'm always so impressed to see the creativity behind a production, especially when a true story based on a book comes to life. It's a beautiful thing when art inspires art!

Julie Perine stars as the Grandmother.

Julie Perine – *"Grandmother"*

I was sitting in Heather Mudrick's family room when Jason Campbell handed her a copy of A PROMISE TO ASTRID and told her he was thinking of making a movie based on the touching story of Mike Tourville. It was June of 2018 and the house was festively decorated for Christmas as filming was taking place for MEGAN'S CHRISTMAS MIRACLE. Dean Cain was there, and I was writing about the JC Films project for the Bridgeport, WV news Website Connect-Bridgeport.com. Just a couple of short months later, I was happy to learn that Jason and his company were coming back to our city to begin filming A PROMISE TO ASTRID Heather and I were excitedly chatting one day when she mentioned that I should be in the film. My acting experience had been limited to church plays, but I thought it was a great idea. I contacted Jason and was ultimately given the role of "Grandma." As I read through the script, I loved the storyline the caring, selfless character of Astrid, who would be played by JoAnn Peterson.

I first met JoAnn and much of the cast at a cookout held at Heather's house to launch the first week of the shoot. There was something special about each person I met as it soon became apparent that a family of sorts had been assembled. Each visit to the set brought more of the same atmosphere. At the move-in scene, I got to know my "movie daughter and son-in-law" Luba Hansen and Jeremy Gladen and I adored them both. My real daughter and granddaughter dropped in that day and they both wound up in the scene; helping to unload Mike's blue pickup truck. We carried the same boxes into the house and out again several times as Gary, Brad and Dan did their magic; filming the scene at different angles and even by drone. I never realized all that went into the making of a movie, including important timing issues and attention to detail to keep continuity. I also never realized that playing a very small role in this movie would leave such a big impact on me. Every day, as I live my life in our little community – the one that reminded Jason so much of Astrid's hometown of Chicopee, Massachusetts– I find myself asking the same question as I encounter various

173

situations and folks: "What would Astrid do?" I think many involved in the film share that same feeling and because of that, the making of this movie in our town has left it an even better place.

I closely covered the filming and associated events, including the premiere of MEGAN'S CHRISTMAS MIRACLE, after which the big funeral scene was filmed at Bridgeport United Methodist Church. According to the traffic the pieces generated and the number of people who jumped on board to serve as extras, there was no doubt that our community was very interested and embraced JC Films and this project. And that feeling of community was evident as the church was packed for the premiere and crowd scene. As Dean Cain walked in, stepped into his clergy robe and stepped behind the pulpit to portray Pastor Scott Seabury, we all sat in the pews, elbow-to-elbow and smiling ear to ear. The Rev. Dr. Ken Ramsey of BUMC gave Dean a thumbs up. I have a real feeling that God is giving this film - which illustrates true selfless, anonymous giving and how to put faith in action - his seal of approval, too.

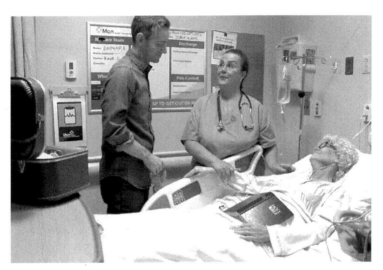

A touching moment as Astrid's time draws short.

Denise Myers stars as Astrid's nurse.

Denise Myers – *Astrid's nurse*

Joann Peterson and I have been friends since being in THE SOUND OF MUSIC together over 12 years ago and she called me about this opportunity. The role was that of an RN, and that is my actual profession, so I felt I would be able to pull it off. Especially since the hospital in which my scene was shot is affiliated with the Health System for which I worked for 30 years! How cool is that?

I have been a nurse in other stage productions, but this was my first time being in a movie. Everyone on the cast and crew were very welcoming and congenial. I only wish I had had more time to be on set with them!

I knew that it was a faith-based story of love, goodness, kindness and generosity, and was glad to be associated with that kind of message! I can identify with Astrid as I, too, believe in angels, and believe that our good works are done best when done silently. I hope this is the first of other opportunities to do Christian movies, but being the first, I must say it was a fascinating, fun experience and an answer to one of my lifelong dreams.

Aaron Lantz stars as the Police Officer.

Aaron Lantz – *"Police Officer"*

In real life I am a full-time police officer, so it was very fitting, and somewhat easy for me to play this role. This was my first time acting, but it came naturally, so it wasn't too straining on my lack of acting ability! My co-workers at the police station jokingly referred to me as "The Movie Star" and "Hollywood" for a while after filming!

Working with the crew was both exciting and a learning experience. While filming my little part, I had the pleasure of getting to speak with some cast and crew. Seeing everyone with different backgrounds, specialties, and ideas coming together to film this movie was awesome!

It was interesting how I came into this role. I walked into the office one morning and my supervisor pointed to me and said, "There is the man for the job!" I had no idea what he was talking about, but when they asked me if I'd like to do it, I said, "Sure, why not?" I was incredibly nervous because I didn't want to screw up my part, even though it was a very small one. Overall, I had a great time doing this and would do it again if the opportunity arose. Anyone listening?

Aaron Lantz has been a police officer with the Bridgeport Police Department for over 5 years.

Keith Hastman stars as Garcia.

Keith Hastman – *"Garcia", Mechanic at Russel's shop*

After seeing a posting for auditions on Facebook and an article in Bridgeport Connect in the summer of 2018, my wife suggested I try out for a part. I thought it was a good story so I gave it a shot. Although I had no previous acting experience, I was interested in knowing how movies were made and working with other people that made movies.

It turned out to be a fun and enjoyable experience, and I made some new friends. Even though my role was small, I learned a lot about making movies, and how much work goes into each scene. I had no idea each scene was run 4-5 times from different angles.

This story teaches you how everyone should be living their lives...very humble and helpful. It teaches you to do good for others and not care about personal recognition. Anyone whose life was touched by Astrid was very fortunate to have her in her life.

Kristen Keeton was the film's Makeup Artist.

Kristen Keeton – *makeup*

My father told me about a film premier at a church in my hometown of Ashland Kentucky. At the premier I met Tim Goodwin and gave him my contact info which he then passed on to Jason. Jason called me a few months later and asked if I would be interested in being the makeup artist for his next project, and I said yes!

This was my very first project and I had never been on an actual film set before! The ASTRID set had an amazing cast and crew! They were all so wonderful to work with, and so patient with a beginner such as myself. I appreciate all of them helping me learn and grow as an artist. Giving me advice and pointers, and even constructive criticism. It was all so helpful!

Every day on set was a brand-new adventure and the set was a blast with everyone's silly antics! One of the funniest/most interesting things though, would have to be Solon wearing hats from the Astrid wardrobe. It was absolutely hysterical!

If you have a dream, it doesn't matter how big it is. It doesn't matter how many people tell you that you can't accomplish that dream, don't listen to them. All you need to do is have faith in The Man Upstairs, believe in yourself, and always continue to work towards your goals!

If some weird kid from a small town can do it by the grace of God, then anyone can.

The real Pastor Scott Seabury.

Scott Seabury

I heard about the book when Mike asked me to preview the book and write an Introduction to it, which I was honored to do.

I heard about the movie when Mike called me in a very memorable phone call to share a series of "You won't believe it, but . . ." statements as he informed me that the book was being made into a movie, and Jason Campbell wrote Pastor Scott Seabury into the script with Dean Cain playing my character. I was thrilled!

What interested me about the movie, aside from Dean Cain assuming my name and other actors playing my family members, was to see Astrid and her story and Mike's words come to life. I was also honored to hear some of the words from my Introduction as part of the eulogy for Astrid in the movie.

I have never worked with the cast and crew before, but I found everyone to be wonderful and talented people, with whom we remain in contact. In the short time we were on set with them, we became a community united in making Astrid's story known.

The book and movie have had a profound effect on me as this has been an exciting and fun chapter of my life and I remain grateful to Mike and Jason for the experience.

The real Cindy Mennard (Tourville).

Cindy Mennard (Tourville)

I was 23 years old when Mike and I moved into the house next door to Astrid. June 4, 1984 to be exact. Astrid and her husband Dominic (Nick as she called him) seemed like a quiet elderly couple that kept to themselves. We were so young, owning our own home, parents of two young sons, Billy and Nicholas, but we thought we were so mature, knowing about life, love and giving. In actuality we were babies with so much to learn. We were a proud young couple trying to do it all on our own.

Sometime during the first year living next door to Astrid we found out we attended the same church in Chicopee, St Christopher's. We always went to the family service at 10:00 and Astrid attended at 8:00 am. I told Father Mike, our pastor at the time, that Astrid gave me a beautiful bouquet of flowers from her garden. He was amazed by that, for her garden was so precious to her, it was truly a very personal gift. I remember thinking how special I felt that she would give me such a gift.

Mike and I kept very busy after we bought the house, Mike worked long hours and I took on various odd jobs to make ends meet. My mom would help care for the boys, so it helped for daycare. Our house was what you would call a fixer upper, so we spent a lot of free time and any spare money wallpapering, painting, and other odd jobs around the house. It was also a time of great joy and fun, as we spent a lot of time with our families and our church friends. My two younger sisters were at our house often and we took them on many excursions with us; the movies (there was an actual drive-in theater in Chicopee at the time and our own little old-fashioned theater called the Rivoli), local fairs, and other day trips. At that time, I also made a lot of my own clothes and outfits for the boys, our nieces and nephews. I even made my sisters prom dresses!

Astrid somehow was very aware of all the activity at 1703 Westover Road! We had many chats over the fence between our homes. It was no surprise that Astrid would notice my car missing and a "For Sale", sign on Mike's truck. She learned of the car accident I was in and our need to replace the car. Soon after, the first monetary gift from Astrid arrived in the form of an old envelope with even older wrinkled up bills inside. I still remember the range of emotions we went through, from disbelief to shock as we were trying to comprehend what had just happened, at six o'clock in the morning, no less, without a word of explanation. It ended up being a little over $1,700! I don't think Mike or I had ever held that much money in our hands at one time, but it had to go back. Well, if you've read this far, you know how it all turned out.

As I reflect on that time and our interaction with Astrid and her gift, I realize that the real gift was Astrid herself, not the money. It was Astrid seeing a young proud struggling family and wanting to help. It was Astrid welcoming me to her home and walking with me through her garden, pointing out her prize possessions. It was Astrid showing us how much she loved and cared for Dominic, her church, and her community.

I still live in the house next door to where Astrid lived, our little fence and her garden are long gone. Astrid would love the couple that live in her house now. Mark and Trish are caring and helpful neighbors.

What has lived on are the life lessons Astrid taught those she helped with her kindness and generosity. She taught us how receive graciously as well as give. As we've learned, Astrid had an impact on many lives, and I'm so happy to see her "come back to life" through the book and the movie.

Mike Tourville

Astrid was an exceptionally private person, and if she were alive today she'd hide from all this attention. She was quite comfortable knowing her discreet - and clever - acts of kindness were simply between her and God, and that's all that mattered. But she did make it interesting—*and* memorable!

In our young lives, Cindy and I were blessed by Astrid's generosity, and by how she restored our faith in people. And now, I feel doubly blessed and incredibly grateful to have worked with such wonderful people on the set of A PROMISE TO ASTRID. Every single person involved. If you've read this far, it's not hard to see that this is a very special group of people. I know Astrid would be proud of their work, and pleased that her simple gestures from so long ago have inspired many to spread goodwill to others in need.

It only takes a small act of kindness to change people's lives and make the world a better place. That's a promise we can all make.

Other cast members:

Carson Campbell	*Billy*
Maddox Mudrick	*Nick (Billy's little brother)*
Maizze Christie	*Lily*
Gabby Christie	*Bryn*
Jamyson Posey	*Nick*
Grace Hansberry	*Kinsley*
Madison Hansberry	*Chelsea*
Emma Hansberry	*Grace*

SPECIAL THANKS

The author and producers would like to thank:

- Ranee Torchia whose house and backyard we used for Mike and Cindy's house, and Connie Arbogast, for allowing us to use her house as Astrid's.
- The City of Bridgeport.
- The Bridgeport Country Club for all the wonderful meals, and special deliveries, for the cast and crew!
- Maple Valley Meats, Bridgeport, WV.
- Chick-Fil-A, Clarksburg, WV.
- Oliverio's Restaurant, Bridgeport, WV.
- Buffalo Wild Wings, Bridgeport, WV.
- Wonderbar Steak House, Clarksburg, WV.
- Holiday Inn Express, Bridgeport, WV.
- Bridgeport United Methodist Church for the church and funeral scenes, and the Bridgeport UMC Choir.
- Stepping Stones Recreation Center.
- Expressions Hair Designs, Bridgeport, WV.
- Dan Cava Auto, Bridgeport, WV.
- Bridgeport Middle School.
- DJ's Diner, Fairmont, WV.
- Ford Funeral Home, Bridgeport, WV.
- Preston Memorial Hospital, Kingwood, WV
- Clarksburg Public Library, Clarksburg, WV.
- Riggs Towing.
- Bridgeport Police and Fire Departments.
- Clarksburg Mission.
- Sanitary Linen Service.

ABOUT THE AUTHOR

Michael K. Tourville lives in Western Massachusetts with his wife Chiara. This is his first book, a true story based on a personal experience that continues to unfold today. Currently, Tourville is the Sales and Marketing Director for Evans Cooling Systems, Inc. based in Connecticut. Mike has two sons, Bill and Nick, a daughter-in-law Angela, and three grandchildren; Lily, Bryn, and Nick.

Reviews for Michael K. Tourville's latest book
Voices from the Fallen:

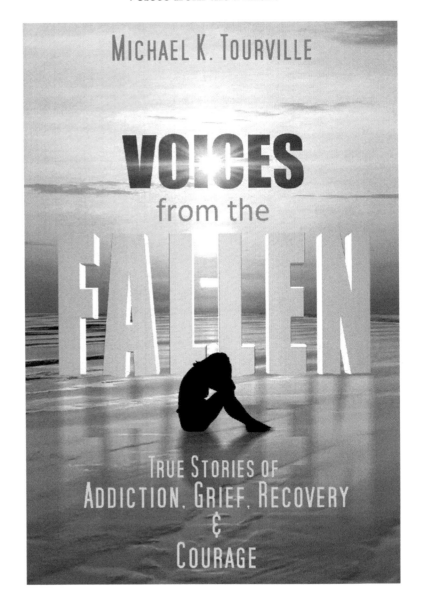

"If, like so many others, you've lost sight of your own life in the drama of tending to someone else's addiction, you may find yourself in this book. Fantastic job taking us into the mind of the addict."

— Dean Cain, Actor, Producer

"Wowzers! When I learned that Mike Tourville was writing a new book, I knew it would be good, but this was amazing. An intense read… I truly felt these stories. My heart was pulled out and put it through the wringer. I seriously was broken reading this."

— Jason Campbell, President, JC Films

"The stories from Voices from the Fallen sadly depict what is real in the world of addiction. This book opens the eyes to the rollercoaster ride for the addicted, as well as the impact on loved ones that must anguish through the daily battle. Mike Tourville illuminates the importance of this problem, which permeates every level of our society. A must read for those personally affected and for anyone educating themselves on the hidden realities."

— Paul Connor, West Springfield Chief of Police

"These hard-hitting experiences are extremely impactful and have the potential to save the lives of those in a similar situation. The extraordinary courage of these individuals and family members to share their personal story with the intent of assisting others goes above and beyond normal expectations. This book is essential reading for those who are at risk or know anyone who may be."

— William Sapelli, Mayor of Agawam, Massachusetts

"This book is a must read for anyone looking for insight and understanding into the life of an addict and those affected by it. The struggle is real and the support available is also real. If you are an addict, or love someone who is suffering from addiction reach out. Remember, you are not alone. There is HOPE!"

—*George and Marilyn Ekimovich, Ministry Leaders,*
LifePoint Church, Chicopee, MA

"Michael Tourville shares the heartbreaking true stories of 8 people devastated by the hell of addiction. They could be our family members, friends, neighbors, or co-workers. In fact, they could be *our* stories. Hopefully, in the reading of these courageous stories, readers will find the strength and compassion to support and help others find healing recovery and renewed life; the productive, loving, fulfilling life that God intends for each of us."

—*The Rev. Scott Seabury*

"This is truly an eye opening and honest read where the author expertly crafts an emotional and painful dialogue between the addict and their loved ones... Each story does a perfect job of showcasing how substance-abuse can happen to anyone, no matter who they are or what their background is. This book helps shine a light on a growing problem within our world, and hopefully we can stop addiction in its tracks before it is too late."

—*Hollywood Book Review*

ALSO AVAILABLE:
A PROMISE TO ASTRID – THE MOVIE

www.AstridFilm.com

Made in the USA
Las Vegas, NV
27 December 2021

39608428R00111